P9-CRX-378

the maine summers cookbook

linda greenlaw and martha greenlaw

the maine summers cookbook

recipes for delicious, sun-filled days

viking studio

641.5974
GRE
4495917

VIKING STUDIO
Published by the Penguin Group
Penguin Group (USA) Inc., 375 Hudson Street, New York, New York 10014, U.S.A.
Penguin Group (Canada), 90 Eglinton Avenue East, Suite 700, Toronto, Ontario,
Canada M4P 2Y3 (a division of Pearson Penguin Canada Inc.)
Penguin Books Ltd, 80 Strand, London WC2R 0RL, England
Penguin Ireland, 25 St. Stephen's Green, Dublin 2, Ireland (a division of Penguin Books Ltd)
Penguin Books Australia Ltd, 250 Camberwell Road, Camberwell, Victoria 3124, Australia
(a division of Pearson Australia Group Pty Ltd)
Penguin Books India Pvt Ltd, 11 Community Centre, Panchsheel Park, New Delhi – 110 017, India
Penguin Group (NZ), 67 Apollo Drive, Rosedale, Auckland 0632, New Zealand (a division of Pearson New Zealand Ltd)
Penguin Books (South Africa) (Pty) Ltd, 24 Sturdee Avenue, Rosebank, Johannesburg 2196, South Africa

Penguin Books Ltd, Registered Offices:
80 Strand, London WC2R 0RL, England

First published in 2011 by Viking Studio,
a member of Penguin Group (USA) Inc.

10 9 8 7 6 5 4 3 2 1

Copyright © Linda Greenlaw and Martha Greenlaw, 2011
All rights reserved

Photographs by Jim Bazin

LIBRARY OF CONGRESS CATALOGING IN PUBLICATION DATA
Greenlaw, Linda.
The Maine summers cookbook : recipes for delicious, sun-filled days / Linda Greenlaw and Martha Greenlaw.
p. cm.
Includes index.
ISBN 978-0-670-02285-4
1. Cooking, American—New England style. 2. Cooking—Maine—Isle au Haut. I. Greenlaw, Martha. II. Title.
TX715.2.N48 G
641.5974—dc22   2011001506

Printed in the United States of America
Set in Helvetica Neue
Designed by Amy Hill

Without limiting the rights under copyright reserved above, no part of this publication may be reproduced,
stored in or introduced into a retrieval system, or transmitted, in any form or by any means (electronic, mechanical,
photocopying, recording or otherwise), without the prior written permission of both the copyright owner and the
above publisher of this book.

The scanning, uploading, and distribution of this book via the Internet or via any other means without the permission
of the publisher is illegal and punishable by law. Please purchase only authorized electronic editions and do not
participate in or encourage electronic piracy of copyrightable materials. Your support of the author's rights is appreciated.

PUBLISHER'S NOTE
The recipes contained in this book are to be followed exactly as written. The publisher is not responsible for your specific
health or allergy needs that may require medical supervision. The publisher is not responsible for any adverse reactions
to the recipes contained in this book.

This book is dedicated to Rhonda.

contents

early in the spring, when thin, crusty strips

of grayish snow still ring the tree trunks, daffodils push proudly up through the newly thawed ground as if they'd been sprung from tight coils. Winters are long on Isle au Haut, and the sudden bursts of yellow amid all of the browns and grays are the first signs that summer is indeed on its way. Fresh yellow, like the sun itself, invokes feelings of warmth and happiness in me. The daffodils are here. My parents will soon arrive. Yay!

Island summers are storybook material. They're that good. Island summers are idyllic, romantic, and fantastic. Sun-filled days of saltwater fun are capped perfectly by colorful sunsets and starry nights that always illicit a contented sigh, as well as goose bumps that rise in answer to the breeze cooled by Penobscot Bay. Our summer island is a paradise for kids, who scramble from tidal pool to tidal pool, buzz around the shore in skiffs, and catch mackerel from the dock. Island summers bring out the kids in all of us, putting a lively spring in even our oldest residents' steps.

Time and place. Island in summer. It's simple. The summer folks show up on the mail boat, the lobsters start to crawl into traps, the gardeners fight the deer for fresh produce, and the parties begin. Food and drink. That's simple, too. Plenty of each. We cook local and fresh, more out of necessity than any heartfelt statement. We just don't have access to gourmet on Isle au Haut. Fortunately for us, our fresh and local includes lobsters, clams, mussels, halibut, blueberries, herbs, and produce that is neither prewashed, double washed, nor even washed at all. We enjoy what the island and surrounding ocean provide. We cook on the beach over open wood fires in washtubs. We boil and steam using seawater dipped from any perch that allows access to the tide. With provisions like these, and a little imagination, meals and their preparations are adventures to be shared and treasured.

My best girlfriend on the island is my mother. When we are together, let there be no question, we are planning our next get-together and assigning who will cook what, where, and how. My mother, even after all these years, is still the boss. Oh, I'll fight her on a few things. But in the end we do it her way. And her way is always a huge success! So after the long, cold winter of sparse ingredients and sparser dinner guests, I can't wait to see those daffodils.

—Linda Greenlaw

summer on the island

Each year my husband Jim and I leave Isle au Haut a couple of days after Thanksgiving and come back around May 15. When we return, there is just no way to describe how happy we are to be back in this wonderful, pristine place.

There are very few people on the island in May, so it gives us a chance to get settled in. Our little island store is open for only a couple of hours for two or three days a week at that time of year, but everyone who is here usually shows up then to buy food or gas, or just to see the people who have spent the winter or who are just back. As the weather warms up, the summer people begin to come over and the store hours are extended. But believe me, if you go to the store as the season gets into full swing, you will see that the line moves very slowly, mostly because everyone is so glad to see one another that they immediately start making plans for events such as dinner parties, sunset cruises, the Point Lookout sailing races, clambakes, the annual pig roast, hikes on the trails, swims in the pond, school fund-raising potluck dinners, weddings, engagement parties, baby showers, and really any other excuse to get together. In high season, property owners here are sure to have company most of the time.

There are a lot of people who I look forward to seeing. I am especially fond of the women of Isle au Haut, who I am proud to say are very strong and self-motivated. These women make our island so unique that I would like to mention a few of them. They are always doing interesting things.

I am going to start with my friend and neighbor Bernadine Barter. For as long as I can remember, Bernie has been in charge of the Fourth of July parade. Just about everyone on the island is a part of it—people decorate their trucks, Jeeps, or whatever they drive to the hilt. Kids ride their bikes or wave from the vehicles. Bernie is also the social director and organizer of our many dances. Billy, her husband, holds our informal island musicals in his workshop. Everyone brings an instrument or his or her singing voice, and we have a great time. Bernie has now taken on the responsibility of meeting every mail boat and acting as the official greeter of people coming over from the mainland. Thank you, Bernie.

Kate Gerteis Shaffer is a first-class chocolatier, and she and her husband, Steve, run a sweet little café called Black Dinah Chocolatiers. They have a Web site, plus Steve sells the chocolate to just about all of the farmers' markets throughout Maine. They are running an up-and-coming business on Isle au Haut.

Diana Santospago runs a wonderful inn on the east side of the island called the Inn at Isle au Haut. She is a *great* cook. She gives you a nice breakfast, packs a nifty lunch so that you can go on hikes or whatever, and provides a dinner meal that is not to be believed—five or six courses, including appetizers and desserts. If you're looking for a great vacation and like to hike, swim, kayak, and fish, this is just the place for you. How about lying in the hammock under a big tree and reading a book?

I would be remiss if I didn't add my daughter Linda to this list of extraordinary Isle au Haut

women. She's a best-selling author and fisherman, as well as a television star. (This is a mother talking.)

Lisa Turner does many things. She is a great cook and caters many social events on the island, including my daughter Biffy and her husband, Ben's, wedding. She is also a teacher's aide at our little island school, where this year we have three children attending.

Now is the time to mention Paula, our schoolteacher. Where would we be without her?

And Dianne (my darling niece), who is the EMT. Believe me, as the island swells over the summer months, she is very busy. Of course she gets backup from our dear friend Nancy Calvert, or "Nurse Nancy." Strong women? Nancy is in a league of her own.

Cathy Fiveash, the island naturalist, knows so much about plants, bushes, trees, birds, bees, and everything else you might be interested in.

Judy Burke ran the Keeper's House Inn, the

island's lighthouse inn, for many years and did a great job of it.

I could and should mention some more strong, island women, but I have probably done all the bragging about our special island that anyone could put up with.

Last, and far from least, is Brenda, the mayor's wife. (Bill is really the first selectman here, but I call him the mayor.) Anyway, Brenda wears many hats: She is the librarian, a big help to her husband, and stern "man" for their boat while Bill's son Nate is out sword fishing with my daughter Linda. These are just a few things that Brenda does. Mostly, she is my good friend. We have a lot of fun together.

Oh, and did I mention our beautiful old-fashioned church, sitting up on a hill overlooking the Thorofare (a body of water that separates Kimball's Island from Isle au Haut)? Jim and I were thrilled when Biffy and Ben decided to have their wedding there.

I hope that this book will entice you to come and see our special little island for yourself. But if you can't, perhaps the recipes within give you the gist of summers on my beloved Isle au Haut.

—*Martha Greenlaw*

cocktails, snacks, and sunsets

white wine–chambord spritzer

This is a refreshing drink on a hot, summer afternoon. —LG

Ice cubes
1½ ounces white wine
1 ounce Chambord
1 teaspoon fresh lime juice
3 ounces chilled club soda
Twist of lime

Fill tall glass with ice cubes. Add the white wine, Chambord, lime juice, and club soda.
Stir gently and garnish with the twist of lime.   Serves 1

martinis with mixed berry simple syrup

I'm not a gin fan. But vodka I like. This martini is refreshing and very pretty in a nice glass. —LG

1½ ounces gin or vodka
¾ ounce dry vermouth
½ teaspoon Mixed Berry Simple Syrup (recipe follows)
Ice cubes
Twist of lemon

Place the gin, dry vermouth, and simple syrup in a cocktail shaker. Shake over ice. Strain into a festive glass and garnish with the twist of lemon.   Serves 1

mixed berry simple syrup

1 cup mixed seasonal berries, such as fresh strawberries and blueberries
1 cup sugar
½ cup water
Juice of 1 lemon

Pulse the berries, sugar, water, and lemon juice in a food processor until the berries are chopped medium. Pour the mixture into a saucepan and simmer over low heat until the sugar is dissolved. Strain out and discard the berry chunks. Chill (see Note).

note: *The syrup can be stored in the refrigerator in a jar with a tight-fitting lid for up to 3 weeks. It can be used to sweeten other drinks or dressings as you desire.*

twenty 2 italiano

There's a new liquor distilled in Maine—Twenty 2 vodka. I joined its Facebook fan page to receive its "3:00 Cocktail" every Friday. (It's a drink recipe, not an actual drink. I wait until 5:00 for that.) Jessica Jewell is the master distiller and has been kind enough to contribute this awesome cocktail recipe. —LG

3 fresh basil leaves
8 fresh oregano leaves
¼ ounce sweet vermouth
1½ ounces Twenty 2 vodka
Ice cubes
Tonic water

Place the basil, oregano, sweet vermouth, and vodka in a cocktail shaker. Fill the shaker with ice cubes. Cover and shake to break up the herbs. Strain the mixture through a wire-mesh sieve into a Collins glass, add fresh ice, and top with tonic water.   Serves 1

not so old-fashioneds

I usually go for the red wine. But every once in a while I think it's good to enjoy what my mother would call a "real drink." Mr. Boston's recipe for an old-fashioned calls for blended whiskey and a cube of sugar. I prefer bourbon and real cherry juice. The tart juice with the orange and lime is nice. The Fresca waters it down a bit for those of us who only dabble in the hard stuff. —LG

1 orange slice
1 lime slice
1 maraschino cherry
1 jigger good-quality bourbon
1 teaspoon sweet vermouth
Dash of bitters
1 teaspoon natural tart cherry juice
Ice cubes
Splash of Fresca

Mash the orange slice, lime slice, and cherry in the bottom of a glass with the back of a small wooden spoon until juicy. Add the bourbon, vermouth, bitters, cherry juice, and ice. Add a splash of Fresca, stir, and enjoy.   Serves 1

strawberry-mint sparkling lemonade

This cocktail has summer written all over it! I'd say July 22 through September 22 is the perfect time for drinking it. Use Twenty 2 vodka only, if you can. This is another recipe from Twenty 2's master distiller, Jessica Jewell. —LG

2 fresh ripe strawberries, hulled
2 tablespoons sugar or sugar substitute
2 ounces Twenty 2 vodka
1 ounce fresh lemon juice
3 fresh mint leaves, plus more for garnish
Ice cubes
3 ounces Fresca

Muddle the strawberries with the sugar in a cocktail shaker, mashing with the back of a spoon until the sugar is dissolved. Add the vodka, lemon juice, and mint. Shake violently for a full 10 seconds. Strain the mixture through a wire-mesh sieve into a glass with ice. Top with Fresca and garnish with more mint leaves.   Serves 1

accidental chips

I have to tell you that when my editor read this recipe she was afraid that someone might actually burn his or her house down trying to produce these chips. Really? So this is a disclaimer: Do not try this at home. It was an "accident," as evident in the title. I usually eat my mistakes and wanted readers to know that I am not perfect, especially in the kitchen. Do I need to add a fire extinguisher to the ingredients list? —LG

½ cup canola oil
4 russet potatoes, scrubbed and sliced very thinly
Coarse salt and freshly ground black pepper

Heat the canola oil in a heavy skillet over high heat until nearly smoking. Scatter the potato slices in the hot oil. Ignore the potato until you smell something burning. Run to the kitchen and frantically turn the potatoes with a long-handled spatula. Allow the potatoes to spatter and sizzle until they look too dark to eat. Remove from the hot oil, drain on paper towels, and season heavily with salt and pepper. Let cool. Chips should be extremely, well, let's say "crisp." Enjoy, being careful of any fragile dental work.   Serves 4

schoolhouse shore clam dip

Schoolhouse shore of Isle au Haut is well known for an abundance of tasty clams. In the summer, my grandchildren love to go to the clam flats, but they often arrive home minus one rubber boot, lost in the soft mud. —MG

10 to 12 freshly dug, soft-shell clams
    (steamers)
One 8-ounce package cream cheese
1 teaspoon Worcestershire sauce
1 pint creamed cottage cheese
10 drops Tabasco sauce
Grated onion and dash of garlic
Clam juice

Rinse the clams in cold water two or three times to remove any sand or grit. Discard any clams that remain open.

Bring a small amount of water to a boil. Add the clams to the water, cover, and steam until the shells open, just a minute or two. Discard any clams that have not opened.

Drain, saving a little of the clam broth. When the clams are cool enough to handle, remove the clams from their shells and discard the shells. Chop the clams finely and add to a bowl with the cream cheese, Worcestershire sauce, cottage cheese, and Tabasco. Season with onion and garlic to taste. Add enough clam broth to make a dipping consistency. Refrigerate for 1 hour or more, stir, and serve with crackers or fresh vegetables. Leftover dip will keep in the refrigerator in a tightly closed container for up to 1 week.   Serves 6 to 8

raw veggies
with spicy yogurt dip

You can obviously make this recipe using whatever veggies you have on hand. Throughout the summer I usually have an assortment of things friends have shared with me from their gardens. This makes for a great low-calorie crudités snack with a cocktail, or a midday "get me through to dinner" treat. —LG

Carrots, cucumbers, cherry tomatoes, summer squash, zucchini, or whatever
vegetables you prefer

for the spicy yogurt dip
1½ cups plain yogurt
¼ cup chopped fresh cilantro
Zest and juice of 1 lime
1 teaspoon Cholula or other hot sauce
2 garlic cloves, minced or crushed
2 teaspoons ancho chili powder

Prepare the vegetables by cleaning, scraping, or peeling as appropriate. Slice or cut into rings or sticks as you desire.

To make the yogurt dip, whisk the yogurt, cilantro, lime zest, lime juice, hot sauce, garlic, and chili powder in a bowl until smooth. Refrigerate in a covered container until ready to serve. It will keep 2 to 3 hours.   Serves 4

creole dipping sauce with green and wax beans

This appetizer, with the green and wax beans, is pretty to look at and healthy for you. It stands out on your buffet table. —MG

for the creole dipping sauce

½ cup vegetable or olive oil

1 small garlic clove, peeled

¼ cup coarsely chopped scallions,
    white and green parts

¼ cup coarsely chopped celery

½ teaspoon salt

¼ teaspoon cayenne pepper

3 drops Tabasco sauce

1½ teaspoons paprika

1 tablespoon ketchup

¼ cup tarragon vinegar

2 tablespoons prepared horseradish

Dijon or other mustard

1 pound wax beans

1 pound green beans

2 tablespoons salt

Several flat-leaf parsley sprigs for garnish

note: *The sauce can be made 2 to 3 days ahead, and the beans can be prepared 1 day ahead. This sauce is also delicious with other vegetables, such as celery and red and green bell pepper strips.*

To make the sauce, place the vegetable oil, garlic, scallions, celery, the ½ teaspoon salt, cayenne, Tobasco, paprika, ketchup, vinegar, horseradish, and mustard in a blender or food processor fitted with a metal blade and process until the mixture is smooth, about 1 minute. Cover and refrigerate (see Note).

To prepare the beans, bring 4 quarts water to a boil. Add the remaining 2 tablespoons salt, and the wax and green beans. Cook until just tender, about 4 minutes. Remove the beans to a colander and rinse under cold water. Drain and pat dry. Cover and refrigerate. Bring the beans to room temperature before serving.

To serve, place the sauce in a small glass bowl on a platter and garnish with parsley sprigs. Arrange the beans in a spoke pattern around the bowl of sauce.   Makes about 2½ cups sauce; 10 servings

sea-salted pita crisps
with garlic-sage hummus

I usually have some goodies on hand for unexpected guests. But one time I had literally just cleaned out my refrigerator and pantry when a couple of friends barged in and insisted that we open a bottle of wine. Well, one bottle led to another, and we got to the point of needing food. I had a large can of chickpeas (garbanzo beans) that had avoided the tossing, and some pita breads were hidden in the freezer. Voilà! —LG

2 tablespoons unsalted butter
2 tablespoons olive oil
6 to 8 fresh pita breads, white or wheat, cut into triangles
Sea salt

for the garlic-sage hummus
One 32-ounce can or two 15-ounce cans chickpeas, rinsed and drained
¼ cup water
¼ cup tahini
Zest and juice of 1 lemon
3 garlic cloves, crushed
3 tablespoons minced fresh sage

Preheat the oven to 375°F.

Melt the butter in a small frying pan over low heat. Add the olive oil and remove the pan from the heat. Brush the pita triangles on one side with the butter and oil and place dry side down on a cookie sheet. Sprinkle with sea salt to taste. Bake until brown and crispy, 8 to 10 minutes.

To make the hummus, place the chickpeas, water, tahini, lemon zest, lemon juice, garlic, and sage in a food processor fitted with a metal blade and pulse until smooth. Transfer to a bowl, cover, and refrigerate until ready to serve. It is best eaten at room temperature.   Serves 4 to 6

smoked salmon spread with rice crackers

One of the surest signs of summer is the arrival of smoked salmon in the Island Store. It reaches us just prior to the first boatload of seasonal residents, and goes immediately into the cooler. We savor it in the weeks to come.

I sometimes double this recipe because of my tendency to sample lots of it before offering it to anyone else. I have become quite an artist in smoothing and re-garnishing the ever-shrinking bowl, making it look as though I haven't dipped in early. —LG

6 ounces smoked salmon

4 ounces cream cheese, softened

2 tablespoons capers, rinsed and drained, plus more for garnish

2 tablespoons minced red onion

1 tablespoon fresh lemon juice

Lemon wedges

1 package rice crackers, preferably wasabi flavored (see Note)

Working with a very sharp knife, cut the salmon into thin strips and then chop the strips into tiny pieces. Mix the salmon and cream cheese in a bowl using the back of a spoon until well blended. Stir in the capers, red onion, and lemon juice. Refrigerate until using, or up to 2 weeks. Bring the spread to room temperature before serving, for ease of spreading. Garnish with additional capers and the lemon wedges. Serve with rice crackers.   Serves 6

note: *If you can't find wasabi-flavored rice crackers, offer your guests a small bit of prepared wasabi in a separate bowl so they can spread it on the crackers if they desire.*

rafting up

Fourth of July 2010 was perhaps the hottest day ever on Isle au Haut. After sweating through the parade in which I was a last-minute, unenthusiastic participant, my sister, Bif, and I wondered what we'd do to celebrate the rest of what has always been my favorite holiday. Cooking on the beach, our usual routine, might amount to severe sunburns. And we knew from experience that once the sun reached a point low enough on the horizon to actually be tolerated, the mosquitoes would come from out of wherever they hide during the day and drive us swatting and swearing inside my house. It seemed the only solution was to organize an impromptu "rafting up."

Rafting up is a blast, plain and simple. "Rafting" is when two boats tie up to each other and share an anchor or mooring. It takes two or more boats, filled beyond legal capacity with fun-loving people who are relaxed enough not to fret about the shortage of life jackets, and a unique spot with a good bottom to set an anchor. Other essentials are beer, food, a grill, an outdoor propane burner, a clam hoe, and fishing rods. Rafting up is basically a floating, clam digging, fishing picnic.

As my sister, Bif, and I departed on foot at the end of the parade route, it became increasingly clear that rafting up would not only be a relief from the heat and bugs, but it would be very well attended. It seemed that no one had much of an organized plan for the rest of this holiday. By the time we reached my driveway, we had five boats and a skiff signed up to meet at the Town Dock at three o'clock that afternoon.

We scurried to collect folding chairs and paper plates, and to fill coolers with ice and then an astonishingly large number of Tupperware containers filled with the remains from my fridge. (Leftovers are welcome in raft-ups.) My brother, Chuck, and brother-in-law, Ben, did the heavier work of getting the gas grill and burner, as well as coolers of drinks, aboard my lobster boat, the *Mattie Belle,* and powering her to the dock in time to receive guests.

There is always a bit of buzz surrounding the preparations for rafting up. Sometimes it's the whispers of an episode in the past when an unnamed partier partied a little too hard but was soon sobered up by an accidental swim. Other times we laugh, remembering scenes such as when my nephew Addison (then six years old) learned to drive the skiff and outboard motor alone. He slowly circled the anchored boats, and we watched until we were dizzy. When the outboard noise became distant, we looked up to see Addison sitting directly on the stem

of the skiff. The outboard motor was going all by itself on the stern—full throttle. Addison had learned that the skiff would go a lot faster with him in the bow! When we finally flagged Addy back to the raft, he received the wrath of all, and then we went back to the business of rafting up.

Addison was demoted back to oars for the remainder of that day. That was funny, I thought now as I drove my loaded truck toward the dock. However, halfway there, and on a sharp turn, another nephew, Aubrey, passed me on the wrong side driving one of my Yamaha scooters, which appeared to be way too big for him.

"See you at the dock, Linny!" Aub said as he whipped by my open window.

It was then that I realized children's safety is measured at the high-water mark here on the island; life jackets below the mark and helmets above the mark. It doesn't matter what they are doing or attempting. My nephews usually leave home early in the morning without eating breakfast. But as long as they have helmets and life vests, we

don't worry. Today, worry was the last thing on our minds. We were going to raft up.

When I arrived at the Town Dock, I was pleased to see the *Mattie Belle* tied alongside and all equipped for cooking. I carried my bags on board and sat with Ben and Chuck on the rail of the boat while they complained about the overwhelming heat and the fact that we'd no doubt be waiting for my mom and dad for a while. It is very unusual to experience heat of this degree so far from the mainland. This was just one of the most odd and infrequent days that offered no breeze. There wasn't even a ripple in the Thorofare. Much to our surprise and delight, my parents soon appeared with their own bags and coolers, and some friends and family stragglers who all climbed aboard. All told, there were fifteen people on board. It was crowded. But there's just no way to turn away a willing guest. (Honestly, when Bif is involved, people show up—her company is that good!) The nephews, and an additional three other island lads, decided they'd meet us in Moore's Harbor with my skiff—in which Aubrey had already claimed the driver's seat. As we tossed the lines and pulled away from the dock, three more friends showed up looking quite forlorn. I yelled to them to wait for the next boat. They smiled and shot thumbs up. I could see Greg Runge aboard *Shockwave,* and knew he'd have room for a few aboard her.

I sat and relaxed on the starboard rail as Chuck drove. The wind in my hair created by our forward motion was like heaven. The boys in the skiff slowly fell behind as they stopped to cast jigs at mackerel on the surface and to haul a few of Aubrey's traps. Good, I thought, we'll have a few lobsters to eat. Behind the boys, *Scalawag,* my friend Simon's boat, soon appeared. I could see quite a crowd aboard *Scalawag* and knew that Simon's family always enjoyed time on the water. And in his wake were Bill and Nancy Calvert, who have a boat of their own and never miss out on a fun adventure. In fact, fun follows Nancy Calvert. This was shaping up to be a great raft!

As we rounded Trial Point and headed toward Deep Cove, a puff of wind blew tiny waves across Penobscot Bay—a promise of the cooling that we all hoped for. When Chuck found a shoal spot with no trap buoys, he dropped the anchor, set it, and secured the line to our bow. The westerly wind was perfect. Simon was soon alongside our port rail and securing to the *Mattie Belle*. Next, my cousin John and his partner, Rick, dallied over to our starboard side and tied their sailboat up to us. They had a boatful of friends, all island summer folks we were happy to see. Next came the Calverts, and

then Greg Runge. There were five boats all told, tethered together and hanging on one anchor. The young boys in the skiff eventually came to our stern, tossed a painter, and climbed aboard the *Mattie Belle*. They were hungry and rightfully assumed that someone would have packed hot dogs.

The grill was fired up as a small group headed ashore to dig a few clams. Teenagers were sprawled on the bows of each boat, sunning and gabbing quietly the way people that age do, seemingly happy to be a part of the party, but separate. When the clam diggers returned with plenty of steamers, the food was in full swing. We had lobster rolls, chicken sandwiches, hot dogs, clams, and steamed lobster with drawn butter, as well as an assortment of snacks and appetizers, that were all passed from boat to boat. Greg Runge cooked clams and lobsters that he served right on the wash

rail of his boat, eliminating the need for platters or plates. People climbed from boat to boat, stopping to eat, have a drink, or just socialize. The boys swam off the stern of *Scalawag* because that boat has a platform for easy, quick exits from icy water. The teenagers weren't far behind in the swim, followed finally by my sister-in-law, Jen. I think we all secretly wanted to plunge in after complaining so about the heat and mugginess ashore. But it was so pleasant there on anchor.

A few of the younger folks had migrated to the roof of the *Mattie Belle*. I'm sure any passerby would envy the scene. We were experiencing sheer joy. Then, from ages eight to eighty (quite literally, Addison to my father), everyone became quiet as the sun rushed the horizon. We had all eaten too much. Some had consumed adult beverages. This Fourth of July was coming to an end too quickly. The sunset was gorgeous with orange and yellow; even pink spilled behind the Camden Hills across Penobscot Bay. There were a few oohs and ahhs, but other than that, we marveled in silence at the sheer breathtaking beauty.

It was time to haul the anchor. Greg cast off and slipped away, followed by Bill Calvert, Simon, and cousin John in his sailboat. The boys buzzed off in the skiff while Chuck weighed anchor and brought up the rear of our tiny fleet. I sat happily on the stern and watched the island slowly pass by.

"Do you really have to leave tonight?" Bif asked.

"Yes, it's time to go," I answered, smiling.

I would get ashore, grab my suitcase, and leave for Stonington, where I would find my Jeep. I had three weeks left in a book-promotion tour, then planned to run home for a day, toss clothes from suitcase to seabag, and go sword fishing for three months.

"Back to work!" I added with a sigh of satisfaction. I love my life, I thought. We would all raft up again next summer.

brenda's famous crab dip

Brenda is a wonderful island friend, with many talents. She is the town librarian and an excellent cook. She serves this, my favorite crab dip, when she entertains, which is quite often. —MG

One and one-half 8-ounce packages cream cheese, softened
2 tablespoons finely chopped onion
1 teaspoon prepared horseradish
1 pound freshly picked crabmeat (more, if desired)
2 tablespoons milk
¼ teaspoon freshly ground black pepper
Dash of paprika

Preheat the oven to 350°F.

Combine the cream cheese, onion, horseradish, crabmeat, milk, and pepper in a bowl. Spoon the mixture into a buttered 8- or 9-inch baking dish and sprinkle with paprika. Bake for about 15 minutes, or until heated thoroughly. Cool slightly. Serve with your favorite crackers. Serves 10 to 12

goat cheese with chives and pimiento on rye crisp breads

Most of my neighbors are Renaissance people who can make many things out of necessity. Someone with one of the more interesting talent combinations is Bill Turner, who built my gorgeous front door and also produces first-rate goat cheese (among other things). —LG

6 ounces good-quality goat cheese,
    such as chèvre
2 tablespoons minced fresh chives
1 tablespoon minced pimiento

for the rye crisp breads
2 tablespoons unsalted butter
2 tablespoons olive oil
1 package party round rye bread
Salt and freshly ground black pepper
    to taste (optional)

Preheat the oven to 350°F.

Blend the goat cheese, chives, and pimiento in a bowl using the back of a spoon. Form the mixture into a log or cup using your hands. Place the log on a serving dish, cover with plastic wrap, and refrigerate before using. The goat cheese can be refrigerated for up to 2 weeks or until the chives are no longer green.

To make the rye crisp breads, melt the butter and olive oil in a saucepan over low heat. Brush one side of the rye rounds and place the rounds, brushed side up, on a cookie sheet. Add salt and pepper, if desired. Bake until crisp. Cool and serve with the goat cheese log.   Serves 12

shrimp remoulade with wickles

I love shrimp remoulade, and I really love Wickles (wicked-good pickles). I think you will agree that Wickles give the shrimp dish a little pizzazz. —MG

1 large egg
1 cup olive oil
2 tablespoons fresh lemon juice
Salt and freshly ground black pepper
1 tablespoon chopped Wickles pickles
1 tablespoon capers, rinsed and drained
2 teaspoons Dijon mustard
1 tablespoon chopped fresh tarragon, plus sprigs for garnish
1 tablespoon chopped fresh flat-leaf parsley, plus sprigs for garnish
2 pounds medium Maine shrimp, peeled (meats only)
Romaine lettuce

Blend together the egg, ¼ cup of the olive oil, the lemon juice, and salt and pepper to taste in a blender or food processor fitted with a metal blade. While the machine is running, add the remaining ¾ cup olive oil in a steady stream until thickened. Mix in the Wickles, capers, mustard, tarragon, and parsley. More herbs, capers, or Wickles can be added to taste.

Bring a large pot of water to a boil. Blanch the shrimp until they turn pink, 1 minute max. Drain and plunge into ice water. Pat dry and chill until ready to use.

Line a large serving platter or individual plates with the romaine. Arrange the shrimp on the lettuce, spoon the sauce over the shrimp, garnish with herb sprigs, and serve. Serves 8

grilled kielbasa
with lemon juice

This is so simple, it's embarrassing. When it was first served to me by my friend Bob Chapman, I thought, "Ya, okay. Gee, Bob, you really went out of your way to feed me here. Really, you heated kielbasa and squeezed lemon over it?" Then I tried it. Now when I serve it, I say it's a secret recipe, so I don't have to admit how little I've done. And let's face it, sometimes when unexpected guests show up at cocktail hour, all you may have is a kielbasa and a lemon on hand. Presto! (When this introduction is longer than the recipe, the recipe is a winner.) —LG

1 pound kielbasa sausage
1 lemon

Prepare the gas or charcoal grill to high heat. Clean and oil the rack (see Note).

Grill the kielbasa, turning frequently, until well browned and sizzling, about 5 minutes. Remove the sausage from the grill and slice it into ½-inch-thick rounds. Place the rounds on a serving platter, squeeze the juice of the lemon all over the sausage rounds, insert toothpicks, and serve warm.   Serves 6

note: *Although I have never broiled kielbasa, I suppose it would be fine. For ease of cleanup, I usually grill things that are greasy and might tend to spatter.*

grilled pineapple
with two dipping sauces

This recipe can be a lot of fun if you make the sauces ahead. It's best served on a picnic table outside, especially if your young nephews are joining you. We learned this the hard way—this snack can be very sticky. It's great to serve with both sauces because they are so completely different but equally delicious. —LG

2 ripe pineapples, peeled, cored, and sliced ¾ inch thick to form rings
Olive oil
Salt and freshly ground black pepper
Fresh Strawberry Sauce (recipe follows)
Ancho Chili Mole Sauce (recipe follows)

Prepare the gas or charcoal grill to medium heat. Clean and oil the rack.

Brush the pineapple rings with olive oil. Salt and pepper to taste.

Grill the pineapple until grill marks appear on it and it is warmed through. Serve with fresh strawberry sauce and ancho chili mole sauce.

fresh strawberry sauce ✝

1 pint (2 cups) fresh strawberries, hulled and coarsely chopped
1 teaspoon pure vanilla extract
2 tablespoons sugar
Juice of 1 lemon
1 cup heavy cream

Place the strawberries, vanilla, sugar, and lemon juice in a blender and pulse until smooth. Add the cream and whip until soft peaks form. Refrigerate until serving.   Makes 3 cups sauce; serves 8

ancho chili mole sauce ✝

½ cup vegetable oil
½ cup raw almonds, chopped
½ cup dry-roasted peanuts
½ cup raisins
¼ cup sesame seeds
2 tablespoons ancho chili powder
1 cup canned plum tomatoes, drained and chopped
3 cups water, plus more if needed
1½ ounces semisweet chocolate, chopped

Heat the vegetable oil in a heavy skillet over medium heat. Sauté the almonds, peanuts, raisins, and sesame seeds for 15 minutes. Transfer to a food processor fitted with a metal blade. Add the chili powder, tomatoes, and 1 cup of the water. Puree until smooth.

Transfer to a heavy medium saucepan and add the remaining 2 cups water. Bring to boil over medium-high heat, whisking constantly. Reduce the heat to low and add the chocolate. Simmer for 15 minutes, whisking until the chocolate is melted and the sauce thickens. Add more water if the sauce becomes too thick. Serve warm with the pineapple for dipping.   Makes 3 cups sauce; serves 8 to 10

chunky chickpea salsa

This is deliciously cool and fresh in the heat of August. I serve it as a dip—it's sort of a lazy way to make hummus. (God knows how I despise washing the food processor.) This salsa is great on fish or chicken, too. —LG

One 15-ounce can chickpeas (garbanzo beans), rinsed, drained, and coarsely chopped
1 garlic clove, minced
Juice of 1 lemon
2 tablespoons extra-virgin olive oil
½ cup diced green bell pepper
½ cup diced red bell pepper
½ cup diced red onion
¼ cup chopped fresh cilantro

Mix together the chickpeas, garlic, lemon juice, olive oil, green bell pepper, red bell pepper, red onion, and cilantro in a medium bowl. Refrigerate until time to serve. Serve with something crunchy, like Sea-Salted Pita Crisps (page 14) or tortilla chips. The salsa can be refrigerated in a tightly sealed plastic container for up to 1 week.   Serves 8

sliced pear and manchego with basil-lime dressing

This is a yummy and relatively healthy alternative to the cheese and crackers that I habitually serve at cocktail hour. —LG

2 ripe Bosc pears, cored and sliced ¼ inch thick
¼ pound good-quality Manchego cheese, sliced ¼ inch thick

for the basil-lime dressing
3 tablespoons extra-virgin olive oil
3 tablespoons minced fresh basil
Zest and juice of 1 lime
½ teaspoon fine sugar or sugar substitute
1 tablespoon plain yogurt or mayonnaise
Shaved carrots or radishes

Alternate the pear and Manchego slices on a serving platter, arranging them so that both are somewhat exposed. Whisk the olive oil, basil, lime zest, lime juice, sugar, and yogurt in a small bowl until well blended. Drizzle the dressing over the fruit and cheese. Garnish with shaved carrots or radishes for a splash of color.   Serves 4

light lunches and suppers for lazy summer days

salads, soups, and sandwiches

fresh pea soup

My daughter, Sarai, was lucky to find a summer job at the Inn at Isle au Haut last year.
She came home one night and announced that she had learned to make soup.
Here it is! —LG

4 tablespoons (½ stick) unsalted butter
2 cups coarsely chopped onions
1 garlic clove, minced
2 pounds sugar snap pea pods, coarsely chopped (or 2 pounds frozen peas)
1 medium potato, peeled and diced small
6 cups chicken broth
1 cup light cream
Salt and freshly ground black pepper

Melt the butter in a large pot over medium heat. Add the onions and garlic, and sauté
until the onions are translucent, about 10 minutes. Add the peas and potato and sauté
for 2 minutes. Add the chicken broth and simmer until the peas and potato are very
tender, about 30 minutes. Cool slightly.

Run the soup through a food mill to remove any strings and skins. Return the soup
to the pot. Stir in the cream and heat gently, being careful not to boil. Add salt and
pepper to taste. Serve hot.   Serves 6

maine shrimp gazpacho

Maine shrimp are extremely delicate and sweet. Although they are a winter fishery, their raw meat freezes wonderfully for use in the summer. Gazpacho is always a winner on a hot day, and with the shrimp it's a bit heartier—more of a meal, but still low calorie and heart healthy. —LG

1½ pounds fresh or fresh-frozen Maine shrimp meat
One 46-ounce jar V8 juice (or tomato juice, if you prefer)
Juice of 1 lime
¼ cup rice vinegar
¼ cup chopped fresh cilantro
¼ cup chopped fresh flat-leaf parsley
1 teaspoon ground cumin
2 chopped ripe medium green tomatoes
2 chopped ripe medium yellow beefsteak tomatoes
1 small red onion, diced
1 medium cucumber, peeled and diced
Salt and freshly ground black pepper
Tabasco sauce

Bring 2 quarts of water to a boil in a heavy saucepan. Add the shrimp meat and stir once. Cook the shrimp for about 1 minute, or until cooked through. Drain in a colander and run cold water over the shrimp to cool quickly. Drain thoroughly.

Place two-thirds of the shrimp in a food processor fitted with a metal blade with enough V8 juice to cover the shrimp. (You may need to do this in stages, depending on the size of the processor.) Pulse until just slightly lumpy. Pour the mixture into a container large enough to hold the remaining ingredients and still fit in the refrigerator. Add the lime juice, vinegar, cilantro, parsley, cumin, green tomatoes, yellow tomatoes, red onion, and cucumber. Stir until blended. Season with salt, pepper, and Tabasco. Cover and refrigerate for about 4 hours. Serve chilled with the remaining one-third shrimp to garnish.   Serves 8

chilled berry soup

Is there anything in the world that is more attractive to look at, or more delicious, than a chilled berry soup on a very warm summer day? Just the idea of fresh Maine blueberries, raspberries, and strawberries in one dish is enough to please anyone. Serving this soup on my deck overlooking Penobscot Bay is the ultimate luncheon experience, in my opinion. —MG

1 cup fresh Maine blueberries

½ cup port wine

1 teaspoon minced fresh ginger

¼ cup light cream

1 cup fresh Maine raspberries

4 cups fresh Maine strawberries, hulled

1 tablespoon chopped fresh mint

2 tablespoons sugar

2 tablespoons white wine vinegar

Fresh mint sprigs

Lemon zest

Orange zest

note: *The soup can be prepared several days before serving.*

Put the blueberries in a food processor fitted with a metal blade and blend until smooth. Strain through a wire-mesh sieve and set aside. Discard the solids.

Bring the port wine and ginger to a boil in a 1-quart saucepan over medium heat. Reduce the heat and simmer for 5 minutes. Add the cream and return to a boil. Cook for 1 minute longer, stirring constantly. Remove the pan from the heat.

Place the reserved blueberries, raspberries, strawberries, mint, sugar, and vinegar in the food processor and process until combined. Add the cream mixture. Process again until well combined. Pour the soup into a container with a tight-fitting lid, cover, and refrigerate until thoroughly chilled, about 4 hours (see Note).

To serve, ladle the chilled soup into thoroughly chilled bowls. Garnish with mint sprigs, lemon zest, and orange zest.   Serves 6

chicken salad sandwiches with lemon and tarragon

These chicken sandwiches are good to take on the boat if we are going to look for whales or puffins, or maybe going to Seal Island to fish for something for dinner that evening. —MG

2 pounds boned cooked chicken, diced
2 small onions, chopped
1 cup diced celery
1½ cups mayonnaise
1 tablespoon fresh tarragon leaves, finely
    snipped
Juice of ½ small lemon
1 tablespoon grated lemon zest
Salt and freshly ground black pepper
16 to 20 slices bread of your choice
    (I like Peggi's bread, toasted; see Note)

Place the chicken, onions, and celery in a food processor fitted with a metal blade and process until smooth. Turn the mixture out into a medium bowl.

Stir together the mayonnaise, tarragon, lemon juice, and lemon zest in a small bowl. Stir well. Add salt and pepper to taste. Pour the mayonnaise mixture over the chicken mixture and mix well.

Spread the chicken salad on half of the bread slices and cover with the remaining slices.   Makes 8 to 10 sandwiches

note: *Peggi Stevens makes wonderful bread that not only tastes good, it is very good for you. She's never shared her recipe, but I can tell you that it is made with whole grains and seeds, among some other good things. I love it toasted. We are lucky to have many great cooks on Isle au Haut.*

veggie sammies

I love sandwiches at any time of year. But on a hot summer day, when vegetable gardens are ripe for the picking, there's nothing more refreshing than a great veggie sandwich. No mayonnaise on this one makes it okay to take on a hike and eat later in the day. I usually can't wait long enough to worry. —LG

8 slices multigrain, healthy, heavy, hearty bread
¼ cup plain hummus (see Note)
1 avocado, pitted, peeled, and thickly sliced
Juice of 1 lime
1 large ripe tomato, thickly sliced
1 red onion, peeled and thickly sliced
4 slices Swiss cheese
1 whole roasted red bell pepper, sliced into thin strips

Spread the top face of the bread slices with hummus. Sprinkle the avocado slices with lime juice and place on 4 pieces of the bread. Top the avocado with tomato, red onion, Swiss cheese slices, and the red pepper strips. Salt and pepper as desired. Close the sandwiches and enjoy. (Am I really describing how to make a sandwich?)   Serves 4

note: *For the hummus, make the Chunky Chickpea Salsa (page 28) for a homemade version.*

maine lobster salad rolls

Lobsters from the cold Atlantic waters are one of the true gastronomical delights. Maine lobsters are considered the very best. As much as I love lobster baked, broiled, steamed, or served as lobster cakes, lobster stew, and in my famous lobster casserole, my favorite lunch in the summer is a lobster roll. If I have friends arriving on the noon boat, you can be sure that they will be having lobster rolls with pickles and chips. —MG

3 cups cooked lobster meat
½ cup finely diced celery
2 teaspoons fresh lemon juice
½ cup mayonnaise
1 tablespoon finely minced fresh dill
Butter for toasting rolls
6 top-split hot dog rolls

Cut the lobster meat into a small dice. Add the celery, lemon juice, and mayonnaise. (The mayonnaise can be mixed half and half with sour cream, if you like.) Add the dill.

Thinly spread a little butter on both sides of the hot dog rolls. Toast the rolls in a large frying pan until they look golden brown and delicious. Fill each roll with the lobster salad.   Serves 6

red crab salad

Crabmeat is a summer staple along the coast of Maine; it is eaten by locals primarily because of its cost relative to lobster. But many people actually prefer crab. To me, it's like comparing apples and oranges—crab and lobster are so different in flavor and texture. I happen to love them both. A new product (to me) is red crabmeat. The red crab is a real success story in the offshore fishing industry, where bad news always gets the press. Atlantic deep-sea red crab is the only domestically harvested crab to have achieved sustainability certification by the Marine Stewardship Council (MSC). The meat is as good as any I have had. And I've had plenty. A nice, fat crabmeat roll on a hot day is refreshing and satisfying. —LG

1½ pounds fresh red crabmeat
    (see Note)
¼ cup diced celery
¼ cup diced yellow bell pepper
3 scallions, green parts only, finely
    chopped
¼ cup plain yogurt
¼ cup mayonnaise
2 tablespoons sour cream
¼ teaspoon sweet Hungarian paprika
1 tablespoon Dijon mustard
Juice of 1 lemon
Freshly ground black pepper

Mix the crabmeat, celery, bell pepper, and scallions in a large bowl until blended. In a separate bowl, whisk together the yogurt, mayonnaise, sour cream, paprika, mustard, and lemon juice until smooth. Add the yogurt mixture to the crab mixture a little at a time until all is mixed, or to desired taste. Grind pepper to taste. Refrigerate until serving. The salad can be enjoyed on top of fresh greens or in a sandwich.   Serves 8

note: *Red crab is worth seeking out, but you can also use regular crabmeat in this recipe.*

grammy getchell's mustard pickles

It was always such a treat for me to visit my grandmother and grandfather Getchell. At the age of seven, I was allowed to go to the post office, take the mail car (I think at a cost of fifteen cents) to Fairfield Center, and be dropped off at my grandparents' house. It was a distance of about five miles and took quite a long time, as we had to stop at every rural mailbox on the way.

My grandmother was usually in the kitchen making pies or frying doughnuts. One particular time she was making mustard pickles. When asked if I could help, she tied one of her aprons around me, and we got to work. I did the heavy looking on, and she made the pickles. I still love mustard pickles, and when we pack a picnic lunch and go on the boat for the day, I always include them. —MG

5 pounds pickling cucumbers, sliced
    into ½-inch-thick rounds
1 cup pickling salt
3½ cups sugar
¾ cup all-purpose flour
½ cup Colman's dry mustard
1½ teaspoons turmeric
1 teaspoon celery seed
4 cups cider vinegar

note: *For the water bath, place a rack in the bottom of a canner. Fill the canner half full with water. Over high heat, bring the water to a full boil. Carefully place the filled jars in the canner far enough apart so the water can circulate freely. Add additional boiling water if needed to come to 1 to 2 inches over the jars. (Do not pour the boiling water over the jars.) Cover the canner and boil gently for 5 minutes (do not start timing until the water reaches the full boil). With a jar lifter or tongs, remove the jars from the canner. Seal the caps as the manufacturer suggests. To cool the jars, place them top side up on a wooden board or folded towels away from drafts.*

Layer the cucumbers and salt in a very large nonmetal bowl. Cover the cucumbers with cold water. Let stand overnight. Drain and rinse well with cold water. Mix the sugar, flour, mustard, turmeric, and celery seed in a large, heavy saucepan. Gradually add the vinegar. Cook and stir until the mixture boils. Add the cucumbers and bring to a boil, stirring constantly to prevent scorching. Pack immediately into 8 to 10 sterilized 16-ounce, wide-mouth Mason jars. Process in a boiling water bath for 5 minutes.   Makes 8 to 10 jars

green salad
with cool guacamole dressing

The success of this recipe is all in the freshness of the greens. Once the lettuces start growing in the local gardens here, I never buy the commercial packaged salads again until the snow starts to fall. My friends Kate and Steve Shaffer (Black Dinah Chocolatiers) host a farmers' market on their lawn every Friday afternoon all summer. The island's gardeners can't keep up with demand for their greens! —LG

1 cup leftover cooked green veggies (green beans, asparagus, broccoli, or any combination)
3 cups assorted fresh salad greens

for the guacamole dressing
1 large ripe avocado, pitted, peeled, and cubed
2 tablespoons plain yogurt
2 tablespoons rice vinegar
1 teaspoon honey mustard
Salt and freshly ground black pepper

Cut the veggies into bite-size pieces and toss with the greens in a large salad bowl.

To make the dressing, place the avocado, yogurt, vinegar, and mustard in a blender and puree until smooth. Salt and generously pepper to taste. Pour the dressing over the salad, toss well, and serve immediately. The dressing can be made 1 day ahead and refrigerated.   Makes ½ to 1 cup dressing, depending on the size of the avocado; serves 6

grilled caesar salad with white anchovy dressing

I don't know where the idea of grilling romaine originated, but the first grilled Caesar I had was at the Inn at Thorn Hill in Jackson, New Hampshire. I was in love (with the salad), and absolutely obsessed with re-creating it. None of my attempts actually failed—it's hard to hurt a Caesar salad—but this is darned close, if not spot-on to the original. I prefer white anchovies to the common variety; they are less salty and fishy. Find them at Italian specialty grocery stores. —LG

6 tablespoons extra-virgin olive oil
2 garlic cloves, minced
6 white anchovy fillets, chopped, plus more fillets for garnish
2 tablespoons fresh lemon juice
2 tablespoons mayonnaise
1 teaspoon whole grain mustard
2 hearts of romaine lettuce, halved lengthwise
Lemon wedges
Salt and freshly ground black pepper

Prepare a medium-hot grill and oil the rack.

Place the olive oil, garlic, anchovies, lemon juice, mayonnaise, and mustard in a food processor fitted with a metal blade and pulse until the anchovy pieces are no longer discernible. Brush the cut sides of the romaine hearts lightly with the anchovy mixture. Place the romaine, cut side down, on the rack and grill until charred in spots and slightly wilted. Serve dressed with the remaining anchovy mixture. Salt and pepper heavily. Garnish with anchovy fillets and lemon wedges. Enjoy!   Serves 4

romaine salad with garlic croutons and asiago

What's better than a homemade crouton? I have a problem saving them for the salad. They're so good hot out of the oven. —LG

1 head garlic, roasted until tender, cloves peeled

2 tablespoons stick unsalted butter

2 cups cubed, day-old sourdough bread

1 large head romaine lettuce

¾ cup good-quality olive oil

¼ cup red wine vinegar

¼ cup minced fresh basil

Salt and freshly ground black pepper

2 tablespoons grated Asiago cheese

Preheat the oven to 350°F.

Sauté the roasted garlic in the butter in a sauté pan over medium heat, stirring to break up the cloves into bits. Toss the bread cubes in the garlic butter to coat evenly. Transfer the cubes in a single layer to a rimmed baking sheet. Bake until golden and crunchy, about 10 minutes. Set aside.

Wash, dry, and gently tear the romaine into bite-size pieces.

Whisk or shake the olive oil, vinegar, basil, and salt and pepper to taste until well blended. Keep the vinaigrette at room temperature and whisk or shake before serving. To serve, put the romaine in a salad bowl, sprinkle with the Asiago, and top with the croutons. Toss it all with the vinaigrette. Because of the fresh basil, I don't keep any leftover vinaigrette.   Serves 4

grilled asparagus salad with chèvre

When my friend Brenda brought me a large bundle of asparagus, I was thrilled. I was at a loss as to what I would serve for a salad. I had cherry tomatoes and cheese, and voilà! The salad was beautiful to look at and tasted really good. —MG

1½ pounds asparagus

Coarse salt and freshly ground black pepper

2 tablespoons plus ½ teaspoon extra-virgin olive oil

2 teaspoons fresh lemon juice

2 tablespoons Dijon mustard

3 to 4 tablespoons snipped fresh chives

6 scallions, including about 2 inches of green, chopped

7 to 8 cups mixed baby salad greens

2 cups red or mixed red and yellow cherry tomatoes, stems removed

4 ounces herbed chèvre, cut into 6 slices

Prepare the gas or charcoal grill to medium-high heat. Clean and oil the rack.

Snap off any tough ends from the asparagus spears and trim the break with a sharp knife. Using a vegetable peeler, and starting just below the tip, peel the skin off each spear, down to the end. Arrange the spears in a single layer on the prepared grill, season with salt and pepper, and drizzle with ½ teaspoon of the olive oil. Grill until tender, 12 to 14 minutes. Transfer to a plate and set aside.

To make a dressing, whisk together the lemon juice, the remaining 2 tablespoons olive oil, and the mustard in a small bowl. Stir in the chives, and season with pepper.

Spoon about 2 tablespoons of the dressing over the asparagus and let stand while tossing the salad greens.

Gently toss together the scallions and salad greens in a large bowl. Add the cherry tomatoes. Drizzle just enough of the dressing onto the salad for the greens to glisten, then toss again. Immediately mound the salad in the center of six large plates. Place a slice of chèvre on top of each mound of greens, and arrange asparagus spears around the perimeter of each plate, dividing them equally. Drizzle a few drops of the remaining dressing over the chèvre. Serve immediately.   Serves 6

carol reynolds's avocado and radish salad

Carol Reynolds and I became fast friends at a late time in our lives. I met her through my son, Chuck, who worked for her son, Michael. Once, when she was visiting on the island, she shared this wonderful recipe with me. The salad is attractive looking, and the radishes are a refreshing contrast in flavor to that of the avocados. Serve this salad as an appetizer or a light lunch, along with an artisanal bread. —MG

24 firm, ripe white radishes (red ones may be substituted)
¾ teaspoon salt
3 ripe avocados
1½ tablespoons minced onion
¾ teaspoon minced chives
1 tablespoon minced fresh flat-leaf parsley
¼ teaspoon freshly ground white pepper
3 tablespoons fresh lemon juice

Scrape the radishes, slice as thinly as possible, and place on a plate. Sprinkle with salt and refrigerate for 30 minutes. Drain off the excess water. Halve, pit, and peel the avocados.

Combine the radishes, onion, chives, parsley, pepper, and lemon juice in a bowl. Mound the mixture equally among the avocado hollows. Serve half an avocado to each person.   Serves 6

grilled zucchini pepper salad

Many people on the island have vegetable gardens, and as you can imagine, there is plenty of zucchini available for anyone who asks. I love this grilled zucchini and pepper salad served with just about anything—hamburgers, steaks, swordfish, chicken. It's all terrific. —MG

1½ pounds zucchini, cut lengthwise into ¼-inch-thick slices
2 red bell peppers, seeded and quartered
¼ cup extra-virgin olive oil
¾ teaspoon salt
⅜ teaspoon freshly ground black pepper
2 tablespoons balsamic vinegar
2 teaspoons light brown sugar
2 tablespoons chopped fresh basil

Prepare the gas or charcoal grill to medium-high heat. Clean and oil the rack.

Toss the zucchini and bell peppers with 2 tablespoons of the olive oil, ½ teaspoon of the salt, and ¼ teaspoon of the pepper. Place the vegetables on an oiled rack and grill, turning occasionally, until tender, 6 to 8 minutes total. Transfer the bell peppers to a bowl and let stand, covered, for 10 minutes. Peel and cut into 1-inch pieces. Cut the zucchini crosswise into 1-inch pieces.

Whisk together the vinegar, brown sugar, the remaining ¼ teaspoon salt, ⅛ teaspoon pepper, and 2 tablespoons olive oil in a large bowl. Stir in the zucchini, bell peppers, and basil. Let stand for 15 minutes for the flavors to blend before serving.   Serves 4

spinach and sprouts salad

This spinach salad is a big hit in my family for lunch or brunch. The crunch in the water chestnuts and bacon adds a lift to the remaining ingredients. All you need to finish this meal is some crusty fresh rolls, and maybe a small dish of fresh fruit on the side. —MG

8 cups spinach, washed and torn into pieces
One 5-ounce can water chestnuts, drained and sliced
1 cup bean sprouts
½ pound fresh white mushrooms, thinly sliced
4 large hard-boiled eggs, coarsely chopped
8 bacon slices, cooked and crumbled, bacon drippings reserved

for the dressing
½ cup extra-virgin olive oil
¼ cup bacon drippings (above)
⅓ cup ketchup
¼ cup red wine vinegar
¼ cup sugar
½ medium onion, grated
1 tablespoon Worcestershire sauce

Toss the spinach, water chestnuts, bean sprouts, mushrooms, eggs, and bacon in a large salad bowl.

To make the dressing, combine the olive oil, bacon drippings, ketchup, vinegar, sugar, onion, and Worcestershire sauce in a saucepan and heat to a simmer.

Pour as much dressing over the salad as desired. Toss and serve at once.   Serves 8

tomato, caramelized onion, and brie galette

Diana at the Inn at Isle au Haut has organized what she calls Culinary Getaways with Island Gourmet Girls on a couple of occasions. The guests who wish to participate have a hands-on dinner party at my place, get cooking instruction at the inn, and make chocolate with our friend and neighbor Kate Gerteis Shaffer of Black Dinah Chocolatiers fame. The last time we did my leg of the culinary journey, Diana prepared this galette in my kitchen. Everyone loved it! —LG

4 tablespoons (½ stick) unsalted butter
2 large onions, thinly sliced
2 garlic cloves, finely minced
Pastry for one 10-inch pie
1 pint grape or cherry tomatoes, halved lengthwise
4 ounces Brie, cubed
Freshly ground black pepper
2 tablespoons finely chopped fresh flat-leaf parsley
1 large egg, well beaten
1 tablespoon grated Parmesan cheese

to make pie pastry
2 cups all-purpose flour
1 teaspoon salt
¾ cup shortening
5 to 6 tablespoons cold water

In a medium-size bowl, sift the flour and salt. With a pastry blender or two knives used scissor fashion, cut in the shortening until the mixture resembles coarse crumbs. Sprinkle cold water 1 tablespoon at a time into the mixture. Mix lightly with a fork until the pastry is just moist enough to hold together. Shape the pastry into a ball. Proceed as directed for a one-bake pie shell or two-baked pie shell.

Preheat the oven to 425°F.

Melt the butter in a large skillet over medium heat. Add the onions and garlic, and sauté until the onions are translucent. Lower the heat, cover the skillet, and cook slowly until caramelized, about 20 minutes.

Line a large cookie sheet with parchment paper. Roll out the pastry to ⅛ inch thickness. Transfer to a rimmed baking sheet. Spread the onions and garlic evenly over the pastry, leaving a narrow border around the edge. Scatter the tomatoes and Brie over the onions. Grind pepper to taste and sprinkle with the parsley. Fold the border up onto the filling and brush with egg. Sprinkle with Parmesan. Bake for 30 minutes, or until golden.   Serves 6

orzo and vegetable salad

My sister-in-law, Jen, brought this salad to a party at my house once. I had never eaten orzo before and really enjoyed it. I ate the leftovers for two days, and I thought the salad got better with age. —LG

2½ cups orzo

1 cup grape tomatoes, halved lengthwise

1 cup sugar snap pea pods, blanched and
    coarsely chopped

½ cup chopped red onion

¼ cup chopped scallions, green parts only

½ cup chopped zucchini

½ cup chopped summer squash

Good-quality olive oil

Salt and freshly ground black pepper

Cook the orzo according to the package directions, drain, and cool completely.

Combine the orzo with the tomatoes, peas, red onion, scallions, zucchini, and summer squash in a large salad bowl. Dress with the olive oil and salt and pepper to taste. Serve at room temperature. The salad stores well in an airtight container in the refrigerator for up to 3 days.   Serves 8

phil brehmer's lobster, blueberry, and asparagus salad

Two of my favorite Maine summer ingredients in one recipe! (I couldn't find a blueberry pie that called for lobster.) Friend and chef Phil Brehmer continues a family tradition of contributing to Greenlaw cookbooks by following in the footsteps of his mother, Ginny Brehmer, who helped with cookbook number one. Thin-stalk asparagus works best for this recipe because it tends to be less stringy than thick-stalk asparagus. —LG

1 pound thin-stalk asparagus

8 cups fresh baby spinach

¼ cup pine nuts, roasted

6 tablespoons extra-virgin olive oil

¼ cup fresh basil, minced

2 tablespoons white balsamic vinegar

Coarse salt and freshly ground black pepper

½ cup fresh Maine blueberries

¼ cup dried cranberries

½ cup halved grape tomatoes

¼ cup diced Bermuda onion

¼ cup diced celery

6 ounces lobster pieces (claw and knuckle meat; tail only, if you wish)

Cut the asparagus stalks back to 6 to 7 inches from the tip. Blanch in a saucepan filled with boiling water for 3 to 4 minutes, drain, and cover with cool water and a few ice cubes. Drain after 10 minutes and chill in the refrigerator for 1 hour.

Rinse and drain the spinach.

Coat the pine nuts with just a few drops of olive oil. Place the pine nuts in a small roasting pan. Place under the broiler (or panfry over medium-high heat) until lightly browned, usually 3 to 4 minutes.

Combine the olive oil, basil, vinegar, a dash of salt, and a dash of pepper in a small bowl. Mix together the blueberries, cranberries, tomatoes, onion, celery, lobster, and pine nuts in a large bowl. Add the vinaigrette and mix well.

To serve, fan your asparagus equally among four plates, placing the tips to the edge. Mix the spinach with the lobster mixture. Ball and center the mixture on the plates over the asparagus. Top with a dash of salt and pepper to taste.   Serves 4

grilled steak salad

Our dear friends Nancy and Bill Calvert summer on Isle au Haut. We don't need much of an excuse to get together at their house, our house, Linny's house, Bif and Ben's, or Chuck and Jen's place for cocktails, dinner, and lots of music. At our last gathering, they shared this steak salad. We all agreed it was a keeper. —MG

for the marinade

¼ cup sunflower oil

2 tablespoons red wine vinegar

1 tablespoon tomato paste

2 teaspoons Worcestershire sauce

1 teaspoon Dijon mustard

1 garlic clove, crushed

½ teaspoon sweet Hungarian paprika

Salt and freshly ground black pepper

———

Four 6-ounce boneless sirloin steaks

for the dressing

1 ripe avocado

Juice of 1 lemon

¼ cup extra-virgin olive oil

1 garlic clove, crushed

¼ cup light cream

Salt and freshly ground black pepper

———

6 cups mixed salad greens

Cherry tomatoes

To make the marinade, put the sunflower oil, vinegar, tomato paste, Worcestershire sauce, mustard, garlic, paprika, and salt and pepper to taste into a large shallow baking dish and mix together. Add the steaks, turn to coat, then set aside for 1 hour.

To make the dressing, halve the avocado, remove the pit, and scoop out the flesh. Place in a blender or food processor fitted with a metal blade with the lemon juice, olive oil, garlic, and cream and process until smooth. Season with salt and pepper (see Note).

Prepare a medium-high grill and oil the rack.

Divide the salad greens among four plates.

Grill the steaks for 6 to 8 minutes, turning once. Transfer the cooked steaks to a board and let rest for 15 minutes. Slice them into strips and arrange them on the plates. Spoon over the dressing and garnish with cherry tomatoes.   Serves 4

note: *The dressing should be used within 2 hours of being made.*

start the day right

brunch egg casserole

The best thing about this egg casserole is the fact that you can make it the day before you wish to serve it. When you are really hungry after an early-morning swim or hike on one of the great trails our island has to offer, this is a perfect dish to serve. —MG

4 tablespoons (½ stick) unsalted butter
¼ cup all-purpose flour
1 cup heavy cream
1 cup milk
¼ teaspoon dried thyme
¼ teaspoon ground marjoram
¼ teaspoon dried basil
1 pound very sharp Cheddar cheese, grated
18 hard-boiled eggs, sliced very thin
1 pound bacon, fried, drained, and crumbled
¼ cup finely chopped flat-leaf parsley
Buttered bread crumbs

Preheat the oven to 350°F.

Melt the butter in a saucepan over medium heat. Gradually stir in the flour, cream, and milk and cook, stirring, until thick. Add the thyme, marjoram, and basil. Add the Cheddar to the sauce, and stir until melted.

Place one-third of the sliced eggs in a layer in the bottom of a large shallow baking dish. Sprinkle one-third of the bacon over the eggs and one-third of the parsley over the bacon. Add a layer of cheese sauce over the eggs, bacon, and parsley. Repeat, making two more layers. Sprinkle with buttered bread crumbs. Bake, uncovered, for 30 minutes, or until slightly golden.   Serves 8

kate's farm stand quiche

I have never made quiche. Why would I, with Kate Shaffer in the neighborhood?
I don't know where she finds time with all she has going on, but Kate's quiche is a
stock item on my breakfast table whenever I have overnight guests. I usually order
enough to have some leftover for lunch after the guests depart. I have always liked
quiche, and this is the best. —LG

for the crust
2¼ cups all-purpose flour
1 teaspoon salt
1 teaspoon sugar
½ pound (2 sticks) cold unsalted butter
¼ to ½ cup ice water

for the filling
4 thick bacon slices
½ onion, thinly sliced
1 cup coarsely chopped baby rainbow chard leaves, including stems
2 cups half-and-half
1 teaspoon salt
⅛ teaspoon freshly grated nutmeg
4 large eggs
¼ cup freshly grated Gruyère cheese

To make the crust, toss the flour, salt, and sugar together in a wide bowl. Using a
hand grater, grate the cold butter directly into the flour mixture, tossing it in as you go.
With cold hands, quickly rub the butter into the flour. Leave some flakes big. Drizzle
in the ice water, mixing briskly with a rubber spatula as you go. When the mixture
is crumbly but moist, stop adding water. Empty the contents of the bowl onto an
unfloured granite slab or wooden board, and finish mixing by smearing and scraping
the dough with the heel of your hand and a bench scraper.

Press the dough together and roll out immediately on a floured surface to a size that will be a fitting crust for the pie plate you are using (a 10-inch deep dish is best). Press into the pie plate, crimp the edges, poke the bottom all over with a fork, and plop the plate into the freezer for a good 30 minutes.

Preheat the oven to 425°F.

Remove the crust from the freezer, line it with aluminum foil, and fill it with dried beans. Bake the crust for 12 minutes. Remove the crust from the oven, and reduce the oven temperature to 350°F.

To make the filling, fry the bacon in a sauté pan over medium-high heat until crisp. Drain on paper towels.

In a clean, lightly oiled sauté pan, cook the onions until just soft, then add the chard. Cover the pan, remove from the heat, and let the vegetables steam while you do the next few steps.

Combine the half-and-half, salt, and nutmeg in a saucepan over medium heat, and stir until it just begins to boil.

In a large bowl, mix the eggs with a whisk, then slowly add the half-and-half mixture in a thin, steady stream, while whisking constantly.

Remove the aluminum foil and beans from the crust. Spread the Gruyère on the bottom of the crust, crumble the bacon on top of the cheese, then spoon the steamed vegetable mixture on top of that. Place the pie plate on a baking sheet. Slowly pour the egg mixture into the crust. Immediately place the quiche on the baking sheet in the oven and bake for 30 minutes, or until the eggs are just set (the quiche will still be a bit wiggly in the middle when the pan is shaken gently).

Remove the quiche from the oven and cool completely before serving. Quiche tastes best when served at room temperature. Really.   Serves 6

blueberry streusel muffins

These are the most indulgent blueberry muffins ever. Bet you will love them. Everyone loves blueberries and probably has a couple of different recipes for them. Have you tried this one yet? It's a winner. —MG

2 cups all-purpose flour

2 teaspoons baking powder

½ teaspoon salt

3 tablespoons sugar

1 large egg

1 cup sour cream

⅓ cup milk

¼ cup vegetable oil

1½ cups fresh blueberries

for the streusel topping

½ cup firmly packed light brown sugar

¼ cup all-purpose flour

1 teaspoon ground cinnamon

3 tablespoons unsalted margarine or butter

Preheat the oven to 425°F. Grease 18 muffin cups with butter.

Sift the flour, baking powder, salt, and sugar together in a large bowl and set aside.

Beat the egg with a whisk until thick. Add the sour cream and milk, and beat to combine. Stir in the vegetable oil. Add the mixture all at once to the flour mixture. Stir only to blend, then fold in the blueberries.

Divide the batter among the muffin cups, filling each three-quarters full.

To make the streusel, stir together the brown sugar, flour, and cinnamon in a medium bowl. Using a pastry cutter or two knives, cut in the margarine until the particles are fine and the mixture is crumbly. Sprinkle the streusel over the batter. Bake for 15 to 20 minutes, or until the tops spring back. Cool slightly and remove from the pan. Allow the muffins to cool for 1 hour before eating, because the berries retain heat.   Makes 18 muffins

black dinah café doughnuts

About her recipe, Kate Gerteis Shaffer writes: "This recipe makes a light, fragrant, and ever-so-slightly chewy doughnut, which has a thin, crispy crust on the outside. The secret, I think, is the egg whites, which give the pastry a fine, yet airy, crumb and eliminates the richness that would otherwise overwhelm the rest of the flavors. I usually refrigerate the batter overnight if possible—this recipe works best when the batter is well chilled." —KS

3½ cups all-purpose flour
1 teaspoon sea salt
1 tablespoon baking powder
1 teaspoon Gingerbread Spice (recipe follows)
3 large egg whites
¾ cup sugar
¼ cup molasses
1 cup buttermilk
½ teaspoon baking soda
1 tablespoon pure vanilla extract
4 tablespoons (½ stick) unsalted butter or margarine, melted, or vegetable oil

———

6 cups vegetable oil, for deep-frying (I use safflower oil)
Sugar and ground cinnamon for finishing the doughnuts

Whisk the flour, sea salt, baking powder, and gingerbread spice together in a large bowl. In another bowl, beat the egg whites, sugar, and molasses with an electric mixer until light colored and creamy. Measure out the buttermilk, then stir the baking soda into the buttermilk to dissolve. Add the buttermilk and baking soda mixture, the vanilla, and the melted butter to the egg white mixture.

Next, add the flour mixture all at once to the egg-buttermilk mixture. Stir to combine. You should have a loose, fragrant batter. Refrigerate until thoroughly chilled. (I usually do this the night before so the batter is ready to fry first thing in the morning.)

Heat the vegetable oil in a large cast-iron skillet until an instant thermometer reads 370°F.

While the oil is heating, flour a board very well. (I use my granite slab—the same one I use for tempering chocolate and rolling out piecrust—because it keeps the batter, now a very soft dough, from warming up and getting too gooey.) Turn the dough out onto the board and gently pat to about ½ inch thickness. Try not to incorporate too much extra flour into the dough. Using a doughnut cutter, cut out as many doughnuts as you can in your first try, then scrape up the dough and pat out once more. After the second cutting, roll any remaining bits of dough into ropes and form round doughnuts that way.

Combine the sugar and cinnamon in a bowl.

Fry the doughnuts, 5 or 6 at a time, until they are golden and cooked through, turning once. Drain on a paper towel–lined baking sheet. Toss them in the cinnamon-scented sugar while they are still warm and place on a cooling rack.

Continue to fry and drain the doughnuts, allowing the oil to come back up to temperature after each batch.

Makes 25 to 30 doughnuts, depending on the size of your doughnut cutter.

gingerbread spice
1 tablespoon ground cinnamon
2 tablespoons ground ginger
1½ teaspoons ground nutmeg
¾ teaspoon ground cloves

Stir together the cinnamon, ginger, nutmeg, and cloves in a small bowl with a small whisk. Store in a tightly sealed jar on the shelf of a cool cupboard.   Makes 24 doughnuts

poached eggs
with mustard hollandaise
sauce

This is Jim's favorite breakfast. Too bad his wife is so lazy! I make it only when we have company. (However, we do have a lot of company throughout the summer, from July through September.) —MG

8 very fresh large eggs
¼ cup white vinegar

for the mustard hollandaise sauce
8 tablespoons (1 stick) unsalted butter
3 large egg yolks, well beaten
1 tablespoon water
1 tablespoon fresh lemon juice
1 teaspoon Dijon mustard
Dash of salt
Dash of white pepper

Break each egg into its own small cup or bowl. Set the cups very near the stove. Fill a deep-frying pan with about 2 inches of water, bring to a boil, then reduce to a simmer before poaching the eggs. Add the vinegar to the water; it helps the eggs hold their shape. Slip the eggs gently into the simmering water by lowering the lip of the cup ½ inch below the surface of the water (see Note). With a slotted spoon, gently nudge the egg whites closer to their yolks. Immediately cover the pan with a lid and turn off the heat. Do not disturb the eggs once you have put them in the water. Set a timer for exactly 3 minutes for medium-firm eggs. Lift each perfectly cooked egg from the water with a slotted spoon after it has cooked to the doneness you want.

To make the sauce, cut the butter into thirds and bring it to room temperature. In the top of a double boiler, combine the egg yolks, water, lemon juice, mustard, salt, and pepper. Add a piece of the butter. Place over boiling water. (The upper pan should not touch the water.) Cook, stirring rapidly with a whisk, until the butter melts and the sauce begins to thicken. Add the remaining butter, a piece at a time, stirring constantly until melted. Continue to cook and stir until the sauce thickens, about 2 minutes more. Immediately remove the top of the double boiler from the heat. If the sauce is too thick or curdles, immediately whisk in 2 tablespoons hot water. Serve over the poached eggs.   Serves 4 to 8

note: *Keep track of which egg went into the water first and remove it first, followed by the rest, in the same order. If you are making eggs for a crowd, cook the eggs ahead of time, slightly undercooking them. Slide them into a large bowl of cold water. When ready to serve, immerse the eggs in barely simmering water for 1 to 2 minutes to warm them.*

delicately thin french pancakes√ with fresh blueberry syrup

When all of our children were growing up, Jim would make these wonderful French pancakes every Sunday. I would mix up the batter for him, and he would prepare them. Today, my son makes them for his two children. Life is good in the Greenlaw family. —MG

2 large eggs
½ cup all-purpose flour
½ cup milk
½ teaspoon salt
2 tablespoons unsalted butter, melted and kept warm

for the blueberry syrup √
1 cup sugar
I tablespoon fresh lemon juice
⅔ cup water
1 pint (2 cups) fresh blueberries

Beat the eggs with a rotary beater in a medium bowl for about 30 seconds. Add the flour, milk, and salt and beat just until blended and smooth. Blend in the melted butter. Let stand, covered, for at least 30 minutes.

Meanwhile, make the blueberry syrup. Combine the sugar, lemon juice, and water in a heavy-bottomed saucepan. Heat gently, stirring until the sugar dissolves. Add the blueberries and bring to a boil. Reduce the heat and simmer until pulpy. Keep warm.

Lightly butter a hot 6- or 7-inch skillet or omelet pan. The butter should sizzle but not brown. Spoon in about 2 tablespoons of the batter and tip the pan to distribute the batter evenly. Cook over a medium heat until brown on one side, about 1 minute, then flip and brown the other side. To serve, spread each pancake thinly with fresh blueberry syrup and roll it up.

Allow 3 pancakes per serving. I love to eat these pancakes with crisp bacon.   Serves 6

ginger-bran blueberry muffins

There is a restaurant in Stonington, Maine—just across from Isle au Haut on the mainland—called the Harbor Café. One day, Jim and I decided to jump on the mail boat and go to the mainland to do some shopping. When we got to Stonington, we were a little hungry, having skipped breakfast. We went to the Harbor Café, where they had just taken ginger-bran blueberry muffins out of the oven. Wow! They were so good. I have been trying to duplicate them ever since. I think this recipe is almost as good. —MG

1 large egg
¼ cup sugar, plus 2 tablespoons for topping
1 cup buttermilk
⅓ cup vegetable oil
¼ cup molasses
1½ cups shredded whole bran cereal
1 cup all-purpose flour
1½ teaspoons baking powder
½ teaspoon baking soda
½ teaspoon ground ginger
¼ teaspoon salt
¼ teaspoon ground cinnamon
¼ teaspoon ground cloves
1½ cups fresh blueberries

Lightly beat the egg with a wire whisk in a medium bowl. Add the ¼ cup sugar, buttermilk, vegetable oil, and molasses and whisk well. Stir in the bran cereal. Let stand for 10 minutes.

Preheat the oven to 375°F. Line 12 muffin cups with paper baking liners.

Combine the flour, baking powder, baking soda, ginger, salt, cinnamon, and cloves in a small bowl and mix well. Add the flour mixture to the bran mixture and mix well. Fold in the blueberries.

Divide the batter evenly among the muffin cups, filling each three-quarters full. Sprinkle each with ½ teaspoon of the additional sugar. Bake for 20 minutes, or until the tops spring back when touched lightly. Cool slightly and remove from the pan. Serve warm or cool.   Makes 12 muffins

feasts with family and friends

starters

mushroom and radish carpaccio with shaved manchego and creamy lemon-pepper drizzle

When a friend who had been visiting the island for a week asked what she could buy me as a little thank-you gift for my hospitality, I didn't hesitate or say it was unnecessary. I wanted a mandoline; not the musical instrument, but the kitchen gadget. That was the beginning of what became "the summer of the mandoline." In this recipe, the mandoline is handy for slicing small mushrooms, radishes—even the cheese. (If you don't own a mandoline, a sharp knife will suffice.) I love raw veggies in the summer! —LG

1 pound large white mushrooms, cleaned

½ pound large radishes, cleaned and ends cut off

1 large head endive

2 ounces Manchego cheese

3 tablespoons extra-virgin olive oil

2 tablespoons fresh lemon juice

1 tablespoon mayonnaise

1 teaspoon coarsely ground black pepper

½ teaspoon honey

Slice the mushrooms and radishes as thin as you can and arrange them on a large serving platter so that they overlap slightly. Shred the endive finely and scatter it over the platter. Shave the Manchego into thin slices and scatter them over the platter.

Blend the olive oil, lemon juice, mayonnaise, pepper, and honey in a small bowl until smooth. Drizzle the dressing over the salad and serve immediately.   Serves 8

maine stuffed clams

This recipe, shared by Eric Prey, is fantastic! Eric is a foodie friend I met through my sister, Bif. If you dig your own or purchase whole clams in the shell, you'll have to shuck them. If you don't know how to do that, simply steam the clams until their shells open a bit. Then pick the meat out and follow the recipe.

Stuffed clams are usually on the menu in the summer months, when we normally get the urge to dig. But one of the most fun times I have had searching for clams was in the winter. My nephews, Aubrey and Addison, were staying with me for their February vacation, and we were looking for adventure. Their friend and fellow islander Jonathan Barter suggested we go to get some hen clams. Here on Isle au Haut, we get them only once or twice a year, when the tide is astronomically low. And in my opinion, the only thing worth doing with hen clams is stuffing them.

Once the boys and I decided to give it a go, the tide was low enough only after dark. We donned headlamps and boots and off we went to Old Cove. We scratched and dug with our hands and old clam shells because we weren't smart enough to bring along any real equipment. We wandered around the snowy shore for hours and had only three clams to show for it. But on this frosty night, they would be comfort food that would remind us that warmer days were coming. —LG

¾ pound (3 sticks) unsalted butter

1 medium onion, finely chopped

3 pounds quahog or surf clam meat

1 medium green bell pepper, seeded and finely chopped

1 medium yellow bell pepper, seeded and finely chopped

1 cup clam juice or clam broth

2 cups panko bread crumbs

1 cup Italian-seasoned bread crumbs

One 7-ounce jar chopped roasted red peppers

1½ cups shredded Monterey Jack cheese

½ cup chopped chorizo sausage

1 tablespoon minced fresh flat-leaf parsley

12 large quahog or surf clam shells, cleaned

1 lemon

Melt the butter in a large pot over medium-high heat. Add the onion and cook for 8 minutes, or until soft. Remove the pot from the heat. Rinse the clam meat in a colander under cold water to remove any grit. Drain the clams well, then mince them. Put them in the pot along with the green bell pepper, yellow bell pepper, and clam juice. Cook for 8 minutes over medium-high heat. Remove from the heat and set aside.

Preheat the oven to 350°F.

Combine the panko bread crumbs, Italian-seasoned bread crumbs, roasted peppers, Monterey Jack, chorizo, and parsley in a large bowl until blended. Add the clam mixture and mix well.

Press the clam stuffing into the clean shells, mounding up the mixture. Place the stuffed shells on a rimmed baking sheet and bake for 25 to 30 minutes, or until hot. Squeeze the juice of the lemon over the hot clams. Serve and enjoy!   Makes 12 stuffed clams

grilled crab-stuffed mushrooms

I first grilled these stuffed mushrooms (normally I would bake them in the oven) on a hot August night when it was too warm to think about cranking up the range. I threw them on the grill and never looked back. —LG

1 pound fresh Maine crabmeat

3 tablespoons mayonnaise

1 tablespoon fresh lemon juice

Dash of Cholula or other hot sauce

½ teaspoon Worcestershire sauce

⅓ cup thoroughly crushed Ritz crackers (optional)

24 large white mushrooms, cleaned, with stems removed

4 tablespoons (½ stick) unsalted butter

Zest of 1 lemon

Prepare the gas or charcoal grill to medium heat. Clean and oil the rack.

Gently mix the crabmeat, mayonnaise, lemon juice, hot sauce, and Worcestershire sauce with a wooden spoon until blended. The mixture should be moist, but not runny. Add mayonnaise or cracker crumbs if needed to obtain the correct stuffing consistency: The stuffing should form firm balls—not be too crumbly. Stuff the mushroom caps with the crab mixture, mounding it as needed to use all the stuffing.

With the grill cover down, grill the stuffed caps, stuffing side up, over medium heat until the mushrooms are brown and the stuffing is hot.

Melt the butter in a small saucepan over low heat. Stir in the lemon zest. Brush or drizzle the lemon butter over the stuffed caps and serve hot.   Makes 24 stuffed mushrooms

seared tuna
with sake-soy reduction
and fried ginger

Seared sushi-grade tuna is one of my signature dishes. Although I usually serve it with wasabi mustard and pickled ginger on the side, I do occasionally get more creative. This variation was born when I had something similar in a restaurant and couldn't coerce the chef to share the recipe. Here's my best guess. And it's amazing! —LG

1 pound fresh sushi-grade tuna steak

1 teaspoon sweet Hungarian paprika

1 teaspoon ground cumin

1 teaspoon sesame seeds (black or white)

½ cup canola oil

Finely chopped fresh chives

for the sake-soy reduction

1 cup sake

¼ cup fine sugar

1 teaspoon whole red peppercorns

2 tablespoons soy sauce

⅓ cup mayonnaise

for the fried ginger

Canola oil for frying

3 tablespoons finely minced fresh ginger

Remove the skin and bloodline (the very dark strip of meat) from the tuna steak. Combine the paprika, cumin, and sesame seeds and rub on the tuna steak, covering all sides evenly.

Heat the canola oil in a medium heavy skillet over medium-high heat until a drop of water spatters on the surface of the hot oil. (The oil should be deep enough to come halfway up the edge of the tuna steak when placed in the pan.) Gently, being careful to not splash the hot oil, place the tuna in the center of the hot skillet and sear for 45 seconds. Carefully turn the steak and sear for another 45 seconds. Quickly remove the tuna from the oil, place on a plate, and put it in the freezer. Allow the tuna to cool in the freezer no longer than 3 or 4 minutes. Remove and wrap and seal tightly in plastic wrap. The tuna can be stored in the refrigerator for up to 3 days.

To make the sake soy, heat the sake, sugar, and peppercorns over medium heat in a small saucepan until the sugar is dissolved. Remove from the heat and ignite the liquid with a kitchen match. Allow the flames to die. Return the pan to the heat and simmer over low heat for 15 minutes to reduce the liquid by about half. Transfer to a bowl and let cool to room temperature. Whisk in the soy sauce and mayonnaise. The reduction can be refrigerated for up to 2 days, but allow it to come to room temperature before using.

To make the fried ginger, heat the canola oil in a small frying pan. Fry the ginger in the hot oil until very brown and crisp. Drain and cool on paper towels.

To serve, slice the tuna thinly across the grain and arrange the slices on a platter. Drizzle with the sake-soy reduction and sprinkle lightly with the fried ginger and chives.   Serves 6

eggplant fritters
with tarragon sour cream

I first met Jen Black Alosa at a fund-raising auction where the first item up for bid—
a cheesecake—went for $2,300. Jen and I agreed that we should start baking, and a
friendship was born. I didn't realize that Jen was a foodie and an accomplished cook
until I saw pictures of her recipes on her Facebook page. She even does her own
photography.

Jen has many fabulous recipes, but this eggplant recipe is one of my favorites.
When I first made these fritters, I grated some zucchini into the batter because I had
a lot of zucchini on hand. I also placed the finished product on beds of baby spinach
because I didn't have watercress. I think you could add any fresh veggies to the batter,
but the fritters are great with just the eggplant. And the spinach worked fine. —LG

3 medium to large eggplants
3 tablespoons olive oil, plus more for rubbing
4 garlic cloves, minced
¼ cup chopped fresh flat-leaf parsley
⅓ cup plain bread crumbs
¼ cup grated Parmesan cheese
2 large eggs, lightly beaten
½ teaspoon ground cumin
½ teaspoon ground coriander
1 teaspoon salt
½ teaspoon freshly ground black pepper
2 bunches watercress

for the tarragon sour cream
1 cup sour cream
1 tablespoon Dijon mustard
½ cup seeded, finely diced cucumber
1 teaspoon minced fresh tarragon
Salt and freshly ground black pepper

Preheat the oven to 450°F.

Cut the eggplants in half lengthwise and rub all over with olive oil. Place the eggplant halves, cut side down, on a rimmed baking sheet. Cook until tender, about 45 minutes. Remove from the oven and let cool until cool enough to handle. Scrape out the flesh with a large spoon and drain in a colander. Discard the skins.

Transfer the eggplant to a large bowl and add the garlic, parsley, bread crumbs, Parmesan, eggs, cumin, coriander, salt, and pepper. Mix thoroughly.

Heat the 3 tablespoons olive oil in a large skillet over medium-high heat. Form 3-inch patties with the eggplant mixture and fry until golden brown, 2 to 3 minutes per side. Remove and drain on paper towels.

To make the tarragon sour cream, whisk together the sour cream, mustard, cucumber, tarragon, and salt and pepper to taste. (You can also make this up to 1 day ahead, refrigerated.)

Place the warm fritters on beds of watercress and top with a nice dollop of tarragon sour cream. Enjoy as an appetizer or an entrée.   Serves 6 as an entrée or 12 as an appetizer

scallops baked in mushroom caps

It was our turn to host the gourmet group on Isle au Haut and we were looking forward to it. Our friends Patty and Dick Ames were in charge of appetizers. They made this wonderful Baked Scallops in Mushroom Caps. They were the hit of the evening. —LG

24 white mushroom caps, cleaned
24 bay scallops, or 8 sea scallops, quartered
8 tablespoons (1 stick) unsalted butter
1 onion, minced
1 or 2 celery stalks, minced
2 garlic cloves, minced
1 teaspoon minced fresh Italian herb (basil, parsley, thyme) blend
1½ cups plain bread crumbs
½ cup grated Parmesan cheese

Preheat the oven to 350°F.

Place the mushroom caps in a single layer, top sides down, on a buttered rimmed baking sheet. Place 1 bay scallop or 1 quarter sea scallop in each cap. Melt 4 tablespoons of the butter in a sauté pan over medium-high heat. Add the onion, celery, and garlic and sauté until tender. Remove from the heat and stir in the herb blend, bread crumbs, and Parmesan. Melt the remaining 4 tablespoons butter.

Stuff the mushroom caps over and around the scallops. Drizzle with the melted butter. Bake for 10 to 12 minutes, or until the mushroom caps are tender and the scallops are cooked.   Makes 24 stuffed mushrooms

artichoke squares

These squares are a favorite in the Greenlaw family and are served as an appetizer, with a salad for lunch, or sometimes at a coffee at the library on Wednesday mornings. —MG

One 12-ounce jar marinated artichoke hearts, saving liquid
1 small onion, finely chopped
¼ cup fine bread crumbs
4 large eggs, lightly beaten
2 cups grated sharp Cheddar cheese
¼ teaspoon salt
⅛ teaspoon freshly ground black pepper
⅛ teaspoon dried oregano
2 tablespoons minced fresh flat-leaf parsley
⅛ teaspoon Tabasco sauce

Preheat the oven to 325°F. Butter an 11×7×2-inch baking pan.

Heat the saved liquid from the artichoke jar in a sauté pan over medium-high heat. Add the onion and sauté until translucent. Finely chop the artichoke hearts. Add the artichoke hearts and bread crumbs to the onions and stir to combine. Add the eggs, Cheddar, salt, pepper, oregano, parsley, and Tabasco, and stir to combine.

Pour the mixture into the prepared pan. Bake for 30 minutes. Remove from the oven and cool slightly before cutting into squares.   Makes thirty-six 2-inch squares

summer veggie spring rolls with garlic-wasabi dipping sauce

From Diana of the Inn at Isle au Haut, these are the epitome of fresh summer goodness. —LG

2 cups shredded green or Napa cabbage

2 cups shredded purple cabbage

1 cup grated carrots

3 cups bean sprouts

½ cup thinly sliced scallions,
    green parts only

⅔ cup chopped fresh cilantro,
    plus unchopped leaves for garnish

Salt and freshly ground black pepper

18 spring roll wrappers (see Note)

2 avocados, pitted, peeled, and sliced;
    slices sprinkled with juice of 1 lemon

½ red bell pepper, seeded and sliced into
    thin strips, plus more for garnish

for the garlic-wasabi dipping sauce

½ cup soy sauce

¼ cup rice vinegar

1 tablespoon hot and spicy garlic oil

1 teaspoon sesame oil

1 garlic clove, finely minced

1 teaspoon wasabi powder

2 tablespoons pickled ginger

2 teaspoons pickled ginger juice

1 scallion, thinly sliced

note: *Spring roll wrappers or rice wrappers can be purchased at most major supermarkets or at Asian or Vietnamese specialty markets. They are found in the refrigerated section with wonton wrappers and fresh noodles. You should also be able to find hot and spicy garlic oil, sesame oil, wasabi powder, and pickled ginger in the Asian section of the supermarket.*

Toss together the green cabbage, purple cabbage, carrots, bean sprouts, scallions, cilantro, and salt and pepper to taste in a large bowl.

In a large pie plate, soften the spring roll wrappers, 5 at a time, in tepid water for 5 minutes. Lay a softened wrapper on a work surface that has been moistened with water. Place an avocado slice, bell pepper strip, and ¼ cup of the veggie mixture on the third of the wrapper closest to you. Pull up the edge of the wrapper closest to you and fold it over the filling. Fold in the sides of the wrapper and roll the wrapper away from you until the spring roll is complete. Repeat to use all the wrappers.

To make the dipping sauce, whisk together the soy sauce, rice vinegar, garlic oil, sesame oil, garlic, wasabi powder, pickled ginger, pickled ginger juice, and scallion in a small bowl. Cover and chill until serving time.

Place a single cilantro leaf on top of each spring roll. Arrange the spring rolls on a platter and garnish with cilantro and red bell pepper strips. Serve with the garlic-wasabi dipping sauce.   Serves 8

baked shrimp
with garlic-basil butter

This shrimp recipe is a well-known dish, served all year-round in Maine. —MG

for the garlic-basil butter

12 tablespoons (1½ sticks) unsalted butter,
    at room temperature

1 teaspoon finely chopped garlic

3 tablespoons finely chopped shallots

½ cup chopped fresh basil

¼ teaspoon salt, or to taste

Freshly ground black pepper

—————

2 pounds large (20 count) shrimp,
    shelled and deveined

Salt and freshly ground black pepper

Basil sprigs

To make the butter, combine the butter, garlic, shallots, basil, salt, and pepper to taste in a mixing bowl and mix well to incorporate. Cover and refrigerate. You can make the butter 1 to 2 days ahead.

Using a little of the garlic-basil butter, grease a large oven-to-table dish. Spread the shrimp evenly in the dish. Season with salt and pepper. Dot the remaining garlic-basil butter evenly over the shrimp. The shrimp can be seasoned and buttered at this point 3 to 4 hours ahead. Cover with plastic wrap and refrigerate. Bring to room temperature 15 minutes before cooking.

When ready to cook the shrimp, preheat the oven to 375°F.

Bake the shrimp, uncovered, on the center rack of the oven until curled and pink, 8 to 10 minutes. Remove from the oven and garnish with the basil sprigs. Serve hot, along with 6-inch wooden skewers.   Serves 8

patty's buttery stuffed shrimp

I love this shrimp appetizer, and because it is so good, I often double the recipe, making enough for two apiece. —MG

1 cup Italian-seasoned bread crumbs
6 tablespoons (¾ stick) unsalted butter, melted
2 tablespoons dry vermouth
1 tablespoon grated Parmesan cheese
1 tablespoon sweet Hungarian paprika
1½ teaspoons minced fresh flat-leaf parsley
1 garlic clove, minced
8 uncooked jumbo shrimp, shelled, deveined, and butterflied
Clarified butter (see Note)

Preheat the oven to 400°F. Butter a large baking pan.

Combine the bread crumbs, butter, dry vermouth, Parmesan, paprika, parsley, and garlic in a large bowl. Arrange the shrimp, cut side up, in the prepared pan. Mound the bread crumb filling atop the shrimp, pressing to compact. Bake until golden brown, 10 to 12 minutes. Serve immediately with clarified butter.   Makes 8 stuffed shrimp

note: *Melt butter in a saucepan over low heat. Remove from heat and let stand for 5 minutes. Skim the foam from the top and discard. Pour the clear butter liquid into a container with a tight-fitting lid. It will keep refrigerated or at room temperature for several weeks or even months. Discard the solids in the bottom of the pan.*

lobster cocktail
with mango cilantro crème fraîche

I have to admit my skepticism on this one. I was once a purist when it came to lobster, wanting it only with drawn butter, and hot. The last couple of summers, the price of lobster has dropped so low that we all started using it as a substitute for other, more expensive ingredients. Lobster has become more versatile in my book. And this is a great, summery starter. —LG

1 pound lobster meat, cut into bite-size pieces

2 lemons, 1 halved and 1 cut into wedges

1 cup crème fraîche

⅓ cup fresh ripe mango, peeled, pitted, and finely diced

¼ cup minced fresh cilantro

½ teaspoon ancho chili powder

Arrange the lobster meat on individual plates and squeeze lemon juice from the lemon halves all over. Put the crème fraîche, mango, cilantro, and chili powder in a food processor fitted with a metal blade and pulse until well blended. Spoon the crème fraîche mixture over the lobster, garnish with the lemon wedges, and serve immediately.   Serves 4

beer-steamed clams
with drawn lemon butter

Digging clams is work for those who do it for a living. For me, it's like therapy. There's something very satisfying about digging into the dirt and pulling out something you can eat. I guess that's the way gardeners feel about their hobby.

Two pounds of steamers will go a long way with non–clam eating people. But if you're feeding clam lovers, keep digging. There are people who absolutely refuse to try clams. More for me! Here, the lemon zest is a small addition with a big "Yes." —LG

2 pounds freshly dug soft-shelled clams (steamers), thoroughly rinsed
½ can (6 ounces) beer
2 cups saltwater (fresh salted water may be substituted)
8 tablespoons (1 stick) unsalted butter
1 lemon

Place the clams in a large kettle. Pour in the beer and water. Cover and place on high heat, steaming the clams until the shells open easily, about 3 minutes.

Melt the butter in a small saucepan over low heat. Zest the lemon into the melted butter.

Shuck the clams, one at a time, from their shells, peeling and discarding the dark covering from the necks. Dip the clam into the hot lemon butter and pop it into your mouth.   Serves 4 to 6

striper ceviche

Striped bass are abundant all along the coast of Maine. They showed up for the first time (that I was aware of) on Isle au Haut just a few summers ago. The fish we catch are relatively small for stripers; we call them schoolies. Their thin fillets are perfect for ceviche. —LG

2 pounds striped bass fillets, skinned and all bones removed

1 cup fresh lime juice with pulp

½ cup peeled and diced jicama

2 garlic cloves, minced

2 tablespoons diced jalapeño from a jar

2 tablespoons minced red onion

½ teaspoon salt

½ teaspoon freshly ground black pepper

¼ cup minced fresh cilantro

Crackers of your choice

Working with a sharp knife, cut the bass into strips about ¼ inch in width. Place in a shallow glass bowl. Pour the lime juice over the bass and give one stir. Add the jicama, garlic, jalapeño, red onion, salt, and pepper. Stir once more, cover, and refrigerate for 30 minutes. Fold in the cilantro and serve with crackers.   Serves 8

roasted oysters

Oysters are always a welcome addition to a party in Maine. On the island we have many great cooks who are always trying to come up with a new recipe to share. This recipe is a little different from the classic roasted oyster preparation. —MG

Coarse salt
6 scallions, including about 2 inches of green, coarsely chopped
1 small head radicchio, coarsely chopped
½ bunch watercress, stems removed
20 large fresh basil leaves, coarsely chopped
2 lemons
2 tablespoons extra-virgin olive oil
1 tablespoon balsamic vinegar
½ cup mayonnaise
Freshly ground black pepper
24 oysters on the half-shell
¼ cup fine plain bread crumbs

Preheat the oven to 500°F. Line a rimmed baking sheet with aluminum foil. Pour in enough salt to form a layer about ½ inch deep and set aside.

Combine the scallions, radicchio, watercress, and basil in a food processor and process until evenly chopped. Set aside.

Grate the zest from 1 of the lemons into a bowl, then juice the lemon, adding the juice to the bowl. Add the olive oil and vinegar and whisk until blended. Whisk in the mayonnaise and season with coarse salt and pepper. Fold in the onion mixture to form a creamy topping.

Using a thin-bladed knife, completely mask each oyster with about 1 tablespoon of the topping. Set the oysters snugly in the salt layer on the baking sheet, allowing space around each one. Sprinkle ½ teaspoon of the bread crumbs over each oyster. Roast until the bread crumbs are lightly browned, 5 to 6 minutes.

When the oysters are ready, divide them among six plates. Cut the remaining lemon into 6 wedges and garnish each serving with a wedge.   Serves 6 mains

stuffed lazy lobster

If you are having ten guests to dinner, and you don't want to deal with lobster shells, lobster juice, tamale, and melted butter all over your best tablecloth, I recommend that you take the time to make this delicious recipe. Everyone loves lobster prepared the lazy way. —MG

1 heaping cup salted pretzel sticks,
    crushed
One 10-ounce can plain bread crumbs
2 teaspoons salt
¼ cup fresh lobster tamale
4 pounds fresh lobster meat
1½ pounds (6 sticks) unsalted butter
½ teaspoon sugar

Preheat the oven to 425°F.

Mix together the crushed pretzels, bread crumbs, 1½ teaspoons of the salt, and the lobster tamale in a medium bowl. Mix until all the lumps disappear.

Cut the lobster meat into bite-size pieces. Heat 1 pound of the butter in a large skillet and add the lobster meat, sugar, and the remaining ½ teaspoon salt. Sauté for 15 minutes, keeping the heat rather low. The liquid will turn rosy yellow.

Divide the hot lobster among twelve 6-ounce ramekins. Place the ramekins in a large broiler pan. Pour the lobster liquid over each dish. Top each with the lobster stuffing. Bake for 10 minutes, or until the stuffing browns. When ready to serve, melt the remaining ½ pound butter and pour it over the browned tops.   Serves 12

grilled lobster
with lime and chile butter

My friends Ann and A.J. served this delicious lobster dish to us the other night. We loved the lime and chile butter flavor. They were kind enough to share the recipe. They visit us every summer for a few days, and we love our time together. They live in Old Lyme, Connecticut, and we met them on the island through mutual friends. We also see a lot of them in Florida, our winter quarters. —MG

8 tablespoons (1 stick) unsalted, softened butter
Grated zest and juice of 1 lime
1 red chile, seeded and very finely chopped
Three 1½-pound lobsters
2 lemons, cut into quarters
Salt and freshly ground black pepper

Prepare the gas or charcoal grill to medium heat. Clean and oil the rack.

Mix the butter with the lime zest, lime juice, and chile. Form the butter into a cylinder, wrap in plastic wrap, and refrigerate to harden.

Cut each lobster in half lengthwise along the back of the shell. Remove the long dark vein and crack the claws.

Squeeze a little lemon juice onto the flesh, sprinkle with salt and pepper to taste, and put the lobsters, flesh side down, on the grill. Turn over the lobsters after 1 minute and cook for another 7 to 8 minutes, until the flesh is white and the shells are red. Put some slices of the lime and chile butter on top of the lobster flesh and allow the butter to melt slightly. Remove the lobsters from the grill and serve with the lemon quarters.   Serves 6

steamed mussels
with pernod and fennel

It's really fun to gather mussels for a meal on a hot summer day. I invented a way of cleaning mussels that I am rather proud of: I put them in a cement mixer with a bit of sea water and tumble them around for twenty minutes. The action of mussel on mussel beats and scrapes off the barnacles and whatever else grows on the outside of their shells. If you don't happen to have a cement mixer among your kitchen gadgets, you can scrape each mussel individually with the edge of another mussel shell. It works great, but it isn't nearly as much fun as the cement mixer. Of course, if you buy mussels from your local fishmonger, they'll already be clean. —LG

8 tablespoons (1 stick) unsalted butter
6 garlic cloves, chopped
1 Vidalia onion, thinly sliced
1 fennel bulb, thinly sliced and fronds chopped
¼ cup Pernod
4 pounds fresh local mussels, scrubbed and beards removed
1 cup chopped fresh flat-leaf parsley
Crusty bread

Melt the butter in a heavy skillet over medium heat. Add the garlic, onion, and fennel and cook until fragrant and beginning to soften. Add the Pernod and remove from the heat.

Place the mussels in a large kettle with a tight-fitting lid. Top with the fennel mixture and the parsley. Cover and steam over high heat until the mussel shells open. Spoon the mussels and veggie bits into four shallow bowls, being sure to share the broth all around. Serve with crusty bread for sopping up the juice. Serves 4

maine shrimp risotto

The shrimp season in Maine is short. So, while the shrimp are in, I use a lot of them. Shrimp freeze well and are a great low-fat summer snack with cocktail sauce. Here, they are more of a comfort food on a cool, foggy night. The spinach and basil really liven up this dish aesthetically. This is one of my go-to recipes when I am expecting Linda Bahnson or Steve Shaffer for dinner. They are both vegetarians who will eat seafood (Linda, only if she's at my place). If that's the standard of vegetarianism, I'm nearly one myself! —LG

2 tablespoons unsalted butter
1 large Vidalia onion, coarsely chopped
1½ cups arborio rice
½ cup dry vermouth
6 cups chicken or veggie broth
1 tablespoon ground cumin
2 tablespoons ancho chili powder
Cholula or other hot sauce
4 cups fresh baby spinach
½ cup coarsely chopped fresh basil
½ cup shredded Parmesan cheese
1 pound fresh Maine shrimp meat

Melt the butter in a large heavy pot over medium-high heat. Add the onion and sauté for 1 minute. Add the rice and stir until completely coated with butter. Add the dry vermouth and continue to stir for 1 more minute. Add the chicken broth, ¾ cup at a time, stirring continually until the liquid is nearly absorbed before adding the next batch. The mixture should be bubbling. When all of the broth has been added (after 45 minutes or so), stir in the cumin, chili powder, and hot sauce to taste. Stir in the spinach in 3 or 4 batches and let wilt. Stir in the basil, Parmesan, and shrimp meat. Remove the pot from the heat and continue to stir until the shrimp meat is cooked through—this will not take long. Serve and enjoy!   Makes 4 hearty servings

red crab cakes two ways

There are so many different crab cake recipes that it boggles my mind. I don't want corn or lemongrass or squash in my crab cake. It's impossible to improve a good crab cake, and sometimes simple is better. This is a standard delicious crab cake that can be dressed any way you might feel like eating it. For the occasions when you need to go a little fancier, I've included the two best toppings I've found (out of hundreds of variations). Both are very different and equally tasty. —LG

1½ pounds North Atlantic red crabmeat, coarsely
    chopped
2 cups panko bread crumbs
2 large eggs, lightly beaten
½ cup mayonnaise
½ cup finely diced celery
½ cup finely diced Vidalia onion
Canola oil for frying
Lemon Tarragon Cream with Maine Blueberries
    (recipe follows)
Fresh Maine Sweet Corn Salsa (recipe follows)

Working with your hands, blend the crabmeat and 1 cup of the panko in a large mixing bowl. Add the eggs, mayonnaise, celery, and onion, and mix with your hands until well blended. The mixture should be quite moist, but not runny. Form patties about the size of hockey pucks, adding more panko or mayonnaise if needed to obtain the desired consistency. Press the patties into the remaining panko, coating both sides, and place them on waxed paper. The patties may be refrigerated at this point for up to 1 day.

Heat the canola oil in a heavy skillet over medium-high heat. Place the patties in the hot skillet in batches, being careful not to crowd the pan. Cook until crisp and brown on both sides, turning once. Remove from the pan and keep hot on a baking sheet in 200°F oven until serving.

Serve with one or both of the following toppings.   Serves 6 to 8

lemon tarragon cream with maine blueberries

4 tablespoons (½ stick) unsalted butter

½ cup minced shallots

1 cup dry white wine

⅔ cup heavy cream

¼ cup minced fresh tarragon

2 tablespoons Pernod

Grated zest of 1 lemon

½ cup fresh Maine blueberries

Melt 2 tablespoons of the butter in a small skillet over medium heat. Add the shallots and sauté for 3 minutes. Add the white wine and boil until the mixture is reduced by half, about 3 minutes. Add the cream, tarragon, and Pernod. Simmer until the sauce is thick enough to cling to the back of a spoon. Spoon the warm sauce over the hot crab cakes and top with the lemon zest and blueberries.

fresh maine sweet corn salsa

3 ears fresh Maine sweet corn, shucked, cooked, and kernels cut from the cob

1 cup canned black beans

¼ cup coarsely chopped fresh cilantro

¼ cup diced red onion

1 ripe tomato, diced

¼ cup diced scallions, green parts only

1 teaspoon ancho chili powder

2 tablespoons red wine vinegar

Combine the corn, black beans, cilantro, red onion, tomato, scallions, chili powder, and vinegar in a mixing bowl. Refrigerate until serving with hot crab cakes. The sauce can be refrigerated in an airtight container for up to 1 week.   Serves 6 to 8

pan-seared sea scallops with roasted red pepper cream sauce

We get big, sweet scallops just offshore of Isle au Haut. I have two friends who fish for scallops and deliver them to my door the same day. Can't get much fresher than that! This recipe is kindly shared by Diana of the Inn at Isle au Haut. —LG

3 tablespoons unsalted butter
1 medium onion, finely chopped
1 garlic clove, minced
1 whole roasted red bell pepper, peeled, seeded, and finely chopped
½ teaspoon coarse salt, plus more to taste
Freshly ground black pepper
1 cup light cream
1 teaspoon fresh lemon juice
1 tablespoon olive oil
1½ pounds fresh local sea scallops
Lemon wedges
Chopped fresh flat-leaf parsley

Heat 2 tablespoons of the butter in a small saucepan over medium heat. Add the onion, garlic, bell pepper, salt, and black pepper to taste. Sauté until the onion is soft and starts to color. Add the cream and lemon juice, reduce the heat to low, and simmer until slightly reduced and thickened, about 5 minutes. Remove from the heat, cool slightly, and puree in a food processor fitted with a metal blade until smooth.

Melt the remaining 1 tablespoon butter with the olive oil in a large skillet over high heat. Season the scallops with salt and pepper. Sear the scallops for 30 seconds per side, turning only once. Transfer to a serving platter and spoon over the roasted red pepper cream sauce. Garnish with lemon wedges and chopped parsley.   Serves 4

grilled swordfish kebabs with peanut-ginger dipping sauce

I originally created this sauce to go over chicken. It was so good that I tried it with swordfish, too. Home run! The kebabs here are all swordfish because I happened to have plenty. If you need to stretch, add chunks of veggies. —LG

for the peanut-ginger dipping sauce

1 tablespoon olive oil

2 tablespoons minced fresh ginger

½ cup creamy peanut butter

¼ cup chicken broth

¼ cup unsweetened coconut milk

Zest and juice of 1 lime

2 tablespoons good-quality ponzu (see Note)

4 pounds fresh, domestically harvested North Atlantic swordfish (see Note)

Olive oil

Salt and feshly ground black pepper

To make the sauce, heat the olive oil in a medium skillet over medium-low heat. Sauté the ginger until very fragrant, about 2 to 3 minutes. Lower the heat to a simmer and add the peanut butter, chicken broth, coconut milk, lime zest, lime juice, and ponzu. Whisk constantly until very smooth. Remove from the heat and let cool. The sauce can be made ahead and refrigerated until ready to use. It's best to warm the sauce before using.

Prepare the gas or charcoal grill to high heat. Clean and oil the rack.

Cut the swordfish into cubes about 2 inches square. Generously oil, salt, and pepper the cubes. Place the swordfish cubes on 8 skewers, dividing the pieces evenly. Grill, turning the skewers to brown all sides of the swordfish, until cooked through. This should take about 12 minutes. Place the skewers on a platter and serve with warmed peanut-ginger dipping sauce.   Serves 8

note: *Good news, fish eaters! The North Atlantic swordfish stock is at 100 percent maximum sustainable yield. The rebuilding is due largely to the efforts of U.S. fishermen. So please always insist on domestically harvested fish. For this recipe, you may need to purchase the fish as a "chunk," which is what fishermen call a section of a loin of any steak fish that has not been sliced into steaks.*

Ponzu is a citrus-based sauce commonly used in Japanese cooking. It is available at Asian specialty markets.

blackened swordfish
with blueberry chutney

We cook outside in the summer as much as possible. And when blackening swordfish properly, the great outdoors is mandatory. I have a propane-fired cooking base that I originally bought to deep-fry a turkey. (That was fun, once.) Now I use the cooker base to hold a gigantic cast-iron frying pan gifted to me by my sister-in-law, who inherited it from her grandfather. The combination of the big BTU burner, the cast-iron skillet, and the right spices and very fresh fish makes this dish a show-stopper—awesome with this blueberry chutney. —LG

for the blueberry chutney

1 teaspoon ground cumin

2 teaspoons finely minced ancho chile pepper

¼ teaspoon salt

2 small, fresh pickling cucumbers, peeled and chopped

3 tablespoons fresh lime juice

3 tablespoons minced fresh flat-leaf parsley

3 tablespoons minced fresh cilantro

1 pint (2 cups) fresh Maine blueberries

Cold water

2 tablespoons ground cumin

2 tablespoons hot paprika

2 tablespoons sesame seeds

1 tablespoon freshly ground black pepper

4 fresh domestically harvested North American swordfish steaks

3 tablespoons canola oil

To make the chutney, toast the cumin, ancho chile, and salt in a small skillet over high heat until fragrant. Set aside and allow to cool completely. Mix the cucumber, lime juice, parsley, cilantro, and cooled spices In a medium bowl. Puree half of the

blueberries in a food processor fitted with a metal blade, adding just enough water to result in a runny consistency. Add the pureed blueberries to the cucumber mixture. Gently fold in the remaining blueberries, being careful to not mash them. Refrigerate until ready to use. (The chutney is best eaten at room temperature over hot fish.)

Mix the cumin, paprika, sesame seeds, and black pepper on a rimmed baking sheet or piece of aluminum foil, spreading the mixture out to thinly cover the surface. Place the swordfish steaks onto the spices, lift them, and turn them over to coat both sides of the swordfish. Rub the spices over the swordfish with your hands to evenly distribute, if needed.

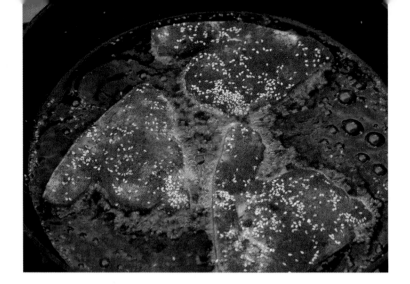

Heat the canola oil in a large heavy skillet (preferably cast iron) over high heat until sizzling hot. Place the swordfish in the hot skillet and cook, turning once, about 3 minutes per side. (Cooking time depends on the thickness of the steak.) The truest test for doneness is to pull the skin from the edge of the steak. If the skin comes off easily, it's done. Swordfish, in my opinion, is not good rare. It should be cooked through, but not dried out. Serve with the blueberry chutney on the side.   Serves 4

flounder florentine

Flounder is a lovely, delicate fish and can be served in many ways. This recipe is nice with fresh Orange Rice with Almonds (page 171) and a simple green salad. —MG

2 pounds chopped fresh spinach (or two 10-ounce packages frozen spinach), cooked and drained
6 flounder fillets (about 1½ pounds)
3 tablespoons unsalted butter
2 tablespoons all-purpose flour
1½ cups milk
Grated Parmesan cheese
Salt and freshly ground black pepper

Preheat the oven to 350°F.

Spread the cooked spinach on the bottom of a large, broiler-proof baking dish. Arrange the fillets on top. Melt the butter in the top of a double boiler. Add the flour and stir to blend. Slowly add the milk, stirring to a thin white sauce consistency. Add enough Parmesan for a medium-thick consistency, stirring until smooth. Season with salt and pepper.

Pour the sauce over the fish. Bake for 20 minutes. Turn on the broiler and broil for an additional 3 to 5 minutes to brown lightly.   Makes six 1-fillet servings

nancy's salmon
with hot mustard glaze

Our friends Nancy and Bob Chapman invited us to dinner one evening. They served this salmon, and we loved it. Of course, I had to have the recipe. I called Harbor Fish Market and told them I needed two pounds of their best center-cut salmon fillet, two inches thick. When buying salmon, choose a fillet that is unbroken, firm-fleshed, moist, and not slimy, and most of all, it should not smell fishy.

Because I live on an island, if I decide I need some incredible fish that is not available locally, I call Harbor Fish Market. I know that they will send me the best there is. I guess what I am saying is, know your fishmonger! —MG

½ cup Colman's dry mustard
½ cup sugar
½ cup water
2 pounds center-cut salmon fillet, about 2 inches thick, with skin
2½ tablespoons extra-virgin olive oil

Preheat the oven to 250°F.

Whisk the mustard, sugar, and water together in a small bowl. Set aside.

Cut the salmon into 4 uniform portions. Pat dry. Heat 1 tablespoon of the olive oil in a heavy ovenproof skillet over high heat; the skillet should be large enough to hold the salmon pieces without crowding. Add the salmon, skin side up, and quickly sear for about 2 minutes, until the pieces can be lifted easily with a spatula without sticking. Turn skin side down and sear for about 2 minutes. The thickest part should still be raw in the center.

Brush the tops of the salmon with the remaining olive oil, and then with the mustard mixture. Place in the oven and cook for about 20 minutes, or until medium-rare in the center. (An instant-read thermometer inserted into the thickest part should register 100° to 110°F.) Remove from the oven and serve.   Serves 4

coconut panko cod
with mexi tartar sauce

This is my answer to coconut shrimp. I first made it for a spontaneous Cinco de Mayo party. I had plenty of cod and not much in the way of anything that might be considered Mexican. Everyone loved it!

The cod can be cut into smaller pieces if you want to serve it as an appetizer. Garnish with lime wedges. —LG

for the mexi tartar sauce

1 cup mayonnaise

1 tablespoon ancho chili powder

1 tablespoon minced jalapeño pepper

Zest and juice of 1 lime

2 garlic cloves, crushed

2 pounds fresh cod fillets

Canola oil for frying

Panko Japanese bread crumbs

Dried shredded coconut

All-purpose flour

2 large eggs beaten with 2 teaspoons unsweetened coconut milk

To make the tartar sauce, whisk together the mayonnaise, chili powder, jalapeño, lime zest, lime juice, and garlic. Refrigerate until serving.

Cut the cod fillets into serving-size pieces. In a heavy skillet, heat enough canola oil to be 2 inches deep and not overrun the edge of the pan when frying the fish. Combine equal parts panko and coconut and roll the cod in the mixture. Dredge the cod in flour and dip in the beaten eggs. Fry the cod in the hot oil until golden and cooked through, turning the fish to brown both sides. (Cooking time will vary with the thickness of the cod fillets.) Serves 6

halibut with herb sauce

When cooked, halibut is a clean, white fish with a mild flavor. If you have guests who are not used to eating fish, this is a good one to start with. —LG

6 tablespoons fresh lemon juice
8 tablespoons extra-virgin olive oil
3 tablespoons chopped fresh basil
3 tablespoons chopped fresh chives
3 tablespoons chopped fresh parsley
Salt and freshly ground black pepper
Six 6-ounce halibut fillets

Preheat the broiler (see Note).

Puree the lemon juice, 6 tablespoons of the olive oil, the basil, chives, and parsley in a food processor fitted with a metal blade. Season with salt and pepper.

Brush the halibut fillets with the remaining 2 tablespoons olive oil. Sprinkle with salt and pepper to taste. Broil until just opaque in the center, about 5 minutes per side. Transfer the halibut to plates. Spoon the herb sauce over and serve.   Serves 6

note: *You can also grill the halibut over medium-high heat. Brush the fish with olive oil, place on a hot grill, and grill for about 5 minutes on each side, or until opaque in the center.*

pulled barbecued chicken ✓
with vidalia onions

I made this pulled chicken to take to a Western-themed party (even wore a cowboy hat!). The best thing about this low and slow method is that you can actually perform other jobs while you're cooking. This is a welcome addition to any function where many people are contributing dishes, and is a delicious leftover in a sandwich. Serve warm with rolls and cole slaw. —LG

3 pounds boneless, skinless chicken breasts and/or thighs
2 large Vidalia onions, sliced ½ inch thick
1 cup chicken broth
1 cup ketchup
⅓ cup firmly packed light brown sugar
4 garlic cloves, minced
½ cup cider vinegar
¼ cup Cholula or other hot sauce
½ cup cola

Preheat the oven to 250° to 300°F.

Place the chicken and onions in a large Dutch oven.

In a separate saucepan, combine the chicken broth, ketchup, brown sugar, garlic, vinegar, hot sauce, and cola over medium heat, stirring until well blended and the brown sugar is dissolved. Pour the mixture over the chicken and onions.

Put a lid on the Dutch oven and bake in the center of the oven at very low heat for 6 hours. Check the chicken for doneness. It should be falling apart. Pull the chicken pieces to shreds using two forks until all the meat is torn apart.   Serves 8

the best burgers
in the summer

blue cheese burgers
with bourbon–black tea ketchup

This recipe actually began with the ketchup. I was seeing so many amazing variations of homemade ketchups in the many food magazines I read that I decided to create my own. When I got it right, I needed a burger to put it on. I really enjoy burgers slathered in blue cheese dressing. But now I prefer the cheese mixed into the beef before grilling.   —LG

for the bourbon–black tea ketchup
One 6-ounce can tomato paste
1 cup strongly brewed black tea
2 tablespoons bourbon
¼ cup cider vinegar
¼ teaspoon ground allspice
½ tablespoon light brown sugar
2 tablespoons molasses

———

2 pounds lean ground beef
¼ cup Worcestershire sauce
1 cup crumbled blue cheese
Coarsely ground black pepper
Hamburger buns (optional)

Prepare the gas or charcoal grill to medium-high heat. Clean and oil the rack.

To make the ketchup, combine the tomato paste, tea, bourbon, vinegar, allspice, brown sugar, and molasses in a heavy saucepan over medium heat and cook, stirring frequently, until very thick about 20 minutes. Cool before serving with the burgers.

Combine the ground beef, Worcestershire sauce, and blue cheese by hand in a bowl, mixing thoroughly. Form the meat into 4 patties and season both sides generously with pepper. (These are rather large burgers. Divide the mixture into 6 to 8 patties, depending on the size of the appetites.) Grill the burgers to the desired doneness (5 to 8 minutes per side), turning once. Place the patties on buns, if desired, and top with the ketchup.   Serves 4 to 8

ben's spice-rubbed burgers with grilled vegetables

Ben, my son-in-law, makes the best melt-in-your-mouth burgers around. He likes to grill, and it shows. When I asked for the recipe, he grinned and said it was a tough job, but someone had to do it. Just because he knows my aversion to grilling, do you think he has to rub it in? This is a meal that everyone will love. —MG

for the grilled vegetables
1 red or white onion, cut into large chunks
1 red bell pepper, seeded and cut into chunks
1 green bell pepper, seeded and cut into chunks
1 yellow bell pepper, seeded and cut into chunks
Handful of portabella mushrooms, seasoned with salt, freshly ground black pepper, and olive oil.
Rosemary balsamic vinegar

———

2 pounds ground round
Stubb's Spice Rub
Hamburger buns (optional)

Prepare a hot grill and oil the rack.

To make the grilled vegetables, grill the onion, red bell pepper, green bell pepper, yellow bell pepper, and portabella mushrooms over high heat until slightly charred and softened, about 8 minutes. Cool to room temperature. Add a splash of rosemary balsamic vinegar when ready to serve.

Form the meat into 8 patties. Liberally sprinkle the spice rub over both sides of the patties and rub in so that they are completely covered. (According to Ben, this seals in the juices.)

Grill the burgers on high with the lid down, checking frequently that they don't flare up. Cook for about 2 minutes on each side for medium-rare. Place on buns, if desired, and top with the grilled vegetables.   Serves 8

grilled turkey burgers
with tomato-mango chutney

When my younger sister was on a no-beef kick, her husband, Ben, created these awesome burgers. Even staunch beef lovers are happy to eat these, and once you try this chutney, you'll never want ketchup on a burger again. —LG

for the tomato-mango chutney
1 cup chopped tomatoes
½ cup chopped mango
2 tablespoons chopped fresh cilantro
2 tablespoons light brown sugar
2 tablespoons fresh lime juice
3 tablespoons plain yogurt

———

2½ pounds ground turkey
1 cup plain bread crumbs
½ cup mayonnaise
2 teaspoons soy sauce
½ cup chopped scallions, green parts only
½ teaspoon ground cumin
Hamburger bun (optional)

Prepare the gas or charcoal grill to high heat. Clean and oil the rack.

To make the chutney, mix the tomatoes, mango, and cilantro by hand in a bowl. Combine the brown sugar, lime juice, and yogurt in a blender until smooth. Toss the tomato-mango mixture with the yogurt dressing. Refrigerate until ready to serve.

Combine the turkey, bread crumbs, mayonnaise, soy sauce, scallions, and cumin by hand in a large bowl. Form the mixture into 8 patties. Grill over hot coals or high heat for 6 minutes per side. Place on a bun, if desired, and top with the chutney.   Serves 8

pita burgers

These pita burgers are a nice change from a more familiar burger, and the family likes them. I am happy with anything grilled, as long as my grill boys (my son, Chuck, and my son-in-law, Ben) are around. I put it together, and they grill. —MG

2 eggs
1 teaspoon turmeric
1 teaspoon ground cumin
¼ teaspoon cayenne pepper
2 garlic cloves, very finely chopped
2 tablespoons minced onion
2 pounds freshly ground lean lamb
½ cup fresh bread cubes, finely diced
8 pitted green olives, chopped
4 pita breads, halved
1 cucumber, finely diced
½ cup sour cream
Salt and freshly ground black pepper
Lettuce

Prepare the gas or charcoal grill to high heat. Clean and oil the rack.

Beat the eggs with the turmeric, cumin, and cayenne pepper in a large bowl. Stir in the garlic and onion. Add the lamb, bread cubes, and chopped olives to the egg mixture and mix thoroughly.

Form the mixture into 8 patties. Grill the burgers to desired doneness (about 8 minutes per side), turning once. When the burgers are nearly ready, warm the pita breads on the side of the grill rack and combine the cucumber, sour cream, and salt and black pepper to taste.

To serve, open the cut sides of each pita and insert a burger. Garnish with lettuce and a dollop of cucumber topping. Serve wrapped in a paper napkin.   Serves 8

spinach-stuffed pork loin

Our friends Joyce and Tom invited a group of us to their home for dinner. When Tom brought a beautiful pork loin to the table, we were impressed. I asked him immediately if he would share the recipe with me. I have served it many times and have never been disappointed. It gets rave reviews. —MG

for the filling

1 tablespoon olive oil

3 ounces fresh spinach, coarsely chopped

½ cup chopped dried tart cherries

¾ cup cooked wild rice

¾ teaspoon dried sage, crushed

⅓ cup chopped pecans

¾ teaspoon salt

¼ teaspoon freshly ground black pepper

for the pork loin

One 2-pound boneless center pork loin roast

½ teaspoon salt

½ teaspoon freshly ground black pepper

¼ teaspoon ground sage

⅛ teaspoon ground thyme

½ cup apricot jam

3 tablespoons water

Preheat the oven to 325°F.

To make the filling, heat the olive oil over medium heat in a large skillet until hot. Add the spinach and cook until wilted. Transfer to a medium bowl and combine with the dried cherries, wild rice, sage, pecans, salt, and pepper. Set aside.

To make the pork loin, trim off the excess fat from the pork. Cut the pork loin lengthwise to make 2 pieces. Make a shallow cut down the center of the cut side of each of the loin halves to make a flatter surface. Sprinkle the cut surfaces of the meat with the salt, pepper, sage, and thyme. Spread the spinach mixture over the cut side of 1 piece of loin. Place the second piece of the loin on top of the spinach mixture to make a sandwich. Tie securely with kitchen twine in several places.

Place the stuffed roast in a roasting pan. Insert a meat thermometer into the thickest part. Roast for 1 hour, or until the meat thermometer registers 140°F.

Meanwhile, melt the apricot jam and water together in a small saucepan over low heat.

Remove the roast from the oven and brush on about half of the apricot mixture. Return the roast to the oven and continue cooking for 10 to 15 minutes, or until the thermometer registers 150°F. Remove from the oven and brush the roast with the remaining apricot mixture. Cover and let stand for 15 minutes before carving.   Serves 6 to 8

grilled spareribs with Dr Pepper glaze

Before using the Dr Pepper, pour it into a bowl and allow it to stand at room temperature until it is no longer effervescent, about four hours.

Start the meal with a relish platter—maybe some colored peppers, sliced into small strips; a few marinated artichoke hearts; some good cheese and crackers; or anything else that looks good. (Perhaps some black and green olives.) Serve the spareribs with the Roasted New Potato Salad (page 150) and Corn Pudding with Fresh Basil (page 157). What to drink: tall glasses of iced tea or frosty mugs of lager. —MG

Four 12-ounce cans flat Dr Pepper (see headnote)
2 cups cherry jam or preserves
⅔ cup Dijon horseradish mustard
3 tablespoons soy sauce
2 tablespoons malt vinegar or cider vinegar
1 tablespoon Tabasco sauce
7½ pounds well-trimmed pork spareribs (see Note)
Salt and freshly ground black pepper

Position the racks in the top and bottom thirds of the oven and preheat the oven to 325°F.

Boil the Dr Pepper in a large heavy saucepan over medium-high heat until reduced to 1½ cups, about 45 minutes. Stir in the cherry jam, mustard, soy sauce, vinegar, and Tabasco. Reduce the heat to medium and simmer, stirring occasionally, until the mixture is reduced to 2½ cups, about 35 minutes. Transfer the glaze to a large bowl and set aside.

Sprinkle the ribs with salt and pepper to taste. Wrap each rib rack tightly in aluminum foil, enclosing it completely. Divide the foil packets between two rimmed baking sheets. Bake until the ribs are very tender, about 2 hours total, switching the positions of the baking sheets halfway through baking. Cool the ribs slightly in the foil. Pour off any fat from the foil packets.

Prepare the gas or charcoal grill to medium-low heat. Clean and oil the rack.

Cut each rib rack between the bones into individual ribs. Set aside 1 cup of the glaze. Add the ribs to the bowl with the remaining glaze and toss to coat. Grill the ribs until brown and glazed, turning to prevent burning, about 5 minutes total. Serve, passing the reserved glaze separately.   Serves 6

note: *The ribs can be prepared 1 day ahead. Keep them covered in aluminum foil packets in the refrigerator. Remove from the refrigerator and let stand for 1 hour before continuing. The glaze can be made 1 week ahead. Cover and chill. Bring to room temperature before continuing.*

halibut steaks with dill

I like halibut steaks spread with mayonnaise and fresh dill. The fish stays moist and has a really nice flavor. —MG

4 to 6 fresh dill sprigs, plus more for garnish
½ cup mayonnaise
Salt and freshly ground black pepper
Four 1-inch-thick halibut steaks
4 to 6 tablespoons yellow cornmeal

Prepare the gas or charcoal grill to high heat. Clean and oil the rack.

Strip the feathery leaves of dill away from the stem. Mix the leaves with the mayonnaise and season with salt and pepper.

Spread both sides of the halibut steaks with the mayonnaise mixture. Dip into the cornmeal to lightly coat.

Grill the halibut steaks for 10 to 15 minutes, turning once, until the steaks are opaque and flaky when tested with the tip of a sharp knife. The surface of the cooked steaks should be golden brown. Sometimes browning occurs before the steaks are cooked through, in which case, reduce the heat or move the steaks to the edge of the grill to finish cooking. Garnish with fresh dill sprigs.   Serves 4 to 6

moxie island baked steak

This is an absolutely delicious way to serve steak, and it gives the hostess time for a cocktail with her guests (that is, if she has the sides, salad, dessert, etc., together). Smart girl! I usually serve this steak when I have invited guests for steak on the grill and, as they arrive, a summer rain decides to fall. One big boom of thunder and I am ready to have Moxie Island steak. —MG

1 cup ketchup
3 tablespoons Worcestershire sauce
8 tablespoons (1 stick) unsalted butter, melted
1 tablespoon fresh lemon juice
One 3-inch-thick sirloin steak
½ teaspoon salt, plus more to taste
¼ teaspoon freshly ground black pepper, plus more to taste
1 garlic clove, minced
1 large Bermuda onion, sliced medium

Preheat the oven to 350°F.

Combine the ketchup, Worcestershire sauce, butter, and lemon juice in a bowl. Set aside.

Place the steak in a 13x9x2-inch broiler pan or baking dish and brown on one side, about 12 minutes. Season with the salt and pepper. Turn over the steak and season the uncooked side with salt and pepper and garlic. Spread with the ketchup mixture and top with the onion slices. Bake, uncovered, for 45 minutes for a medium-well steak.   Serves 10

wine and pepper steaks

A simple but delicious way to serve steak. —MG

1¼ cups dry red wine
½ cup olive oil
2 tablespoons green peppercorns, ground
2 tablespoons coriander seeds
Eight 1-inch-thick sirloin steaks, trimmed
Fresh cilantro sprigs
Lightly salted whipped cream (optional)

Mix together the red wine, olive oil, ground peppercorns, and coriander seeds in a large bowl.

Prick the steaks deeply, then immerse them in the wine marinade and leave them uncovered at room temperature for at least 2 hours.

Prepare the gas or charcoal grill to high heat. Clean and oil the rack.

Grill the steaks for 1 minute on each side to seal, then continue cooking, turning the steaks occasionally and basting frequently with the marinade until cooked as desired. As a general rule, a rare steak will require 3 to 4 minutes on each side; a medium steak, 6 to 7 minutes; and a well-done steak, 8 to 10 minutes. Garnish the steaks with sprigs of cilantro and serve plain or with a spoonful of lightly salted whipped cream, if desired.   Serves 8

grilled tuscan steak
with sun-dried tomato marinade

The combination of sun-dried tomatoes and fresh basil leaves makes this grilled steak terrific. —MG

½ cup dry red wine
8 to 10 sun-dried tomatoes packed in oil, drained
Handful of fresh basil leaves
3 tablespoons olive oil
4 garlic cloves, chopped
1 teaspoon salt
2 teaspoons freshly ground black pepper
Two 1-inch-thick top round steaks

Mix the red wine, sun-dried tomatoes, basil, olive oil, garlic, salt, and pepper together in a bowl until you have a smooth, thick sauce. Pour into a shallow dish.

Add the steaks to the sun-dried tomato marinade and turn until evenly coated. Cover and place in the refrigerator for 2 hours.

Prepare the gas or charcoal grill to high heat. Clean and oil the rack.

Remove the steaks from the marinade. Grill over high heat, turning once, until desired doneness, 6 to 10 minutes. Discard the marinade.　Serves 2

pig roast

My friend

"Barney" (Dave Bahnson) is perhaps the most interesting man I have ever met. Barney has such an eclectic array of . . . I hesitate to refer to what Barney does beyond his occupation as hobbies, but I don't know how else to define his extracurricular activities. He doesn't just fly; he owns two airplanes. He doesn't dabble in woodworking; he builds gorgeous pieces of furniture. He doesn't collect airplane memorabilia; he is the go-to authority on vintage propellers. Even the Smithsonian defers to Barney. So when Barney said he had built a pig roaster and was willing to donate it to help with a fund-raiser that my mother and I were co-hosting, I got pretty excited.

The roaster rode in the back of a pickup truck from Mendon, Vermont, to Stonington, Maine, where I met it with open arms and wide eyes. What a contraption! Barney had built the thing from a 275-gallon oil tank. It was on big wagon wheels and had a trailer hitch welded to one end, making it somewhat mobile out of the truck. It was equipped with an electric rotisserie, the spit of which was the axle out of one of Barney's old cars and was hooked to a universal joint. The electric motor had a timer that could be tweaked to slow or speed up the rotation of the meat while cooking. The bottom of the body of the roaster was fitted with several adjustable vents that could be twirled open and closed by kicking them with the toe of your shoe. A temperature gauge that appeared to have been snatched from a boiler system stuck out prominently from the top of the cover, which was hinged on the back side for ease of opening and closing. Barney had designed and welded a two-piece, cagelike pig holder that held the entire animal together throughout the spinning and cooking process. When I finally finished my Q and A session and roaster tour with a friend who had come with me, we slung the beast with straps, hoisted it hydraulically aboard the mail boat, and headed to Isle au Haut.

The roaster ended up in my front yard, where we buffed it up with a grinder and sprayed it with cans of black paint. We brushed the wheels with metallic silver and accented them with bright red. We made a tag from an old license plate that read THE BAHNSON BURNER, and it was game on!

We moved the roaster to the event site the day before the actual party, mostly because of the time required to roast a two-hundred-pound pig. (Getting the pig to the island is a story unto itself. Suffice it to say that it did *not* ride on my boat—that is bad luck!) The roaster became the greatest spectacle any of the island residents had seen since the boom truck carrying the frame of my brother's new post-and-beam house went for a swim. Everyone who walked or rode by stopped to check it out. Everyone who stopped

was thoroughly amused with the whole concept, and this raised the hype for the party. Many folks went home to retrieve cameras. Now the pressure was on to produce the delicious, moist, smoky pork as advertised for the three hundred expected attendees.

The job of preparing the pig was quite a chore. The most difficult thing was thawing the pig enough to get the axle pushed through. It seemed the pig had been frozen in a bit of a curled position, prohibiting the shaft from driving through stem to stern. I knew that time was of the essence and, being the take-charge woman that I am, went and got a dingy from the Town Dock. We put the pig in the dinghy and ran a garden hose to it. All of

this in the middle of the field beside the Kennedys' boathouse for all the town to see. The running water did the trick, and the pig was successfully skewered and manhandled into position in the roaster.

Next was the garlic. Barney taught me how to use the trocar (a medical device sometimes inserted into the throat of a dying person to open an airway) and plunger to get umpteen garlic cloves through the tough, thick pigskin (there's a reason they used to make footballs from pigskin). By now, the roaster was circled with lawn chairs filled with interested onlookers who like to drink beer (and offer advice). Once the pig was declared thoroughly studded, it was time to light the match.

The best wood for cooking pork in this fashion is apple wood. It just so happens that there are apple trees on the island, and some of them are readily accessible after dark. An accomplice and I had taken care of appropriating apple wood days before, and a summer resident had also donated boxes of perfectly cut wood that he'd purchased off-island. So when the wood got thrown into one pile, nobody was the wiser, and I never heard any repercussions for our harmless theft.

Once the fire was going in good shape, we established watches. Barney and his wife, Boo, would take the first watch, as they were the only chefs experienced with this particular model of equipment and method. They instructed others who had volunteered how to keep the temperature at a steady 275°F by adding wood, closing and opening vents, and so on. I went home and crashed into bed, leaving the bulk of the overnight duty to my brother and brother-in-law, Chuck and Ben. They are both good cooks and didn't seem to mind staying up all night following Barney and Boo. If they felt the need to sleep, they decided, they were to wake one of the other volunteers for a turn. The guys reasoned that they were on vacation and probably wouldn't have gone to bed even if they weren't responsible for the pig.

The next morning, I rushed toward the field. I couldn't wait to take my watch. The light, northerly breeze held the most delicious, mouthwatering aroma of roast pork. I first smelled it by Billy Barter's shop, and it got stronger as I drove, making me press the gas pedal down a bit farther than I normally would have. When I arrived, there was plenty of discussion around the roaster, including about the fact that Chuck and

Ben had never wakened anyone else to take their turns. It soon became clear that Ben and Chuck had dozed through the night in lawn chairs, waking to find the entire roaster in flames, and then to find the fire completely out, and then . . . So, the temperature had ranged from 500° to 0°F. They reasoned that the average was around the desired 275°F. They were both covered with greasy soot, except for rings around their lips where beer cans had scrubbed them clean. Ben and Chuck were happy to go to their homes, shower, and nap before the big event, leaving me to figure out the pig.

The entire island population was scheduled to show up at noon, so I was worried about the menu, to say the least. Fortunately, Barney and his wife were soon back on the scene, saving me from total despair.

"Don't worry, Linny. You just can't totally ruin these things."

Not totally ruining this wasn't exactly the way I wanted the centerpiece of my party to be described. But, it was too late now. Besides, I knew that everyone would bring side dishes to share, so we wouldn't go hungry. It just seemed like a lot of work to "not totally ruin."

One hour before the crowd descended upon us, Barney flung open the roaster and declared the pig "done." It was black, like charcoal. I couldn't imagine anything less appetizing in appearance. "It's perfect," Barney said before I could suggest rolling it off the end of the Kennedys' dock.

At noon, tables were set up and food arrived in salad bowls, in covered dishes, and on paper plates. A couple of men helped Barney lift the pig from the roaster and onto a table to carve. Barney peeled the black skin from the carcass, exposing some beautiful meat. He began to cut and pile slices onto platters that people could help themselves to in buffet-line fashion. Barney cut and cut and cut, never falling behind the crowd of very impressed diners. When I explained to some of the islanders that Barney's real occupation was as an orthopedic surgeon, there was a lot of surprise and then admiration for the complete anomaly of the man. And the pork was, indeed, "perfect," which Chuck and Ben took full credit for. We've done six more pig roasts since then, and haven't managed to totally ruin one yet.

roast pig, island style

One 200-pound pig, gutted, with head on
10 large garlic heads, cloves separated and peeled
1 trocar with plunger
One 275-gallon oil tank converted to a pig roaster
Four armloads of apple wood, dried and split
1 match
1 fire extinguisher

red sauce for roast pig

8 cups ketchup
2 cups water
Juice of 3 lemons
2 large Vidalia onions, coarsely chopped
1 cup firmly packed light brown sugar
½ cup granulated sugar
1 cup Dijon mustard
1 cup Worcestershire sauce
1 cup cider vinegar

Mix the ketchup, water, lemon juice, onions, brown sugar, granulated sugar, mustard, Worcestershire sauce, and vinegar in a large kettle over medium heat. Cook until nearly boiling, stirring constantly. Reduce the heat to a low simmer and cook for 1 hour, stirring occasionally. The source may be refrigerated until barbecue day. Reheat over low heat and serve hot.   Serves 250

yellow sauce for roast pig

6 cups yellow mustard
2 cups honey
1½ cups cider vinegar
¼ cup firmly packed light brown sugar
3 tablespoons Worcestershire sauce
3 tablespoons ground cumin

Mix the mustard, honey, vinegar, brown sugar, Worcestershire sauce, and cumin in a large kettle over medium heat. Cook until nearly boiling, stirring constantly. Reduce the heat and simmer for 1 hour, stirring occasionally. The sauce may be refrigerated until ready to use. Reheat over low heat and serve hot.   Serves 250

macaroni salad with avocado and olives

Ah, the all-purpose macaroni salad! This is great for picnic, cookout, or lunch at home. Although I have made it only with elbow macaroni, I'm sure it would be as good with any small pasta. —LG

12 ounces elbow macaroni or other pasta
1 large avocado, pitted, peeled, and chopped
½ cup assorted Spanish olives, pitted and chopped
One 8-ounce jar pimientos, drained and chopped
½ cup minced red onion
2 tablespoons extra-virgin olive oil
1 tablespoon fresh lime juice
½ teaspoon sugar or sugar substitute
Freshly ground black pepper

Prepare the macaroni according to package directions. Cook until tender, but still firm. Rinse the macaroni under cold water and drain thoroughly. Place in a large bowl and gently mix the avocado, olives, pimientos, and red onion into the macaroni.

Whisk together the olive oil, lime juice, and sugar in small bowl. Pour the oil mixture over the macaroni mixture and toss to coat. Season with pepper. Refrigerate, covered, until mealtime. Serve cool or at room temperature.   Serves 8

cilantro and cholula corn bread

This is a good bread to serve with a bowl of chili, or black bean soup, or maybe even ribs. —MG

2 large eggs
1 cup buttermilk
1½ cups yellow cornmeal
½ cup all-purpose flour
1 teaspoon salt
1 teaspoon sugar
3 tablespoons vegetable oil
2 tablespoons fresh finely chopped cilantro
1 teaspoon Cholula or other hot sauce
1 teaspoon baking powder
½ teaspoon baking soda

Preheat the oven to 400°F. Oil or grease a 13×9×2-inch baking pan.

Beat the eggs well by hand in a medium bowl. Add the buttermilk, cornmeal, flour, salt, sugar, vegetable oil, cilantro, and Cholula and beat thoroughly. Stir in the baking powder and baking soda, and mix only for a few seconds to blend.

Pour the batter into the prepared pan. Bake for 25 to 30 minutes, or until lightly browned.   Serves 6 to 8

sides

rosemary balsamic roasted red potatoes

These potatoes are really good with steak or a hamburger. —MG

2 tablespoons olive oil

2 pounds small red potatoes, scrubbed and quartered

1 tablespoon finely chopped scallion, green part only

6 garlic cloves, minced

1 teaspoon dried thyme

1 teaspoon ground cumin

¼ cup rosemary balsamic vinegar

Salt and freshly ground black pepper

Preheat the oven to 400°F. Coat a 15×10×1-inch baking pan with nonstick cooking spray.

Heat the olive oil over medium-high heat in a large skillet. Add the potatoes, scallion, and garlic, and toss to combine. Add the thyme and cumin; toss well. Cook and stir for 2 to 3 minutes, or until the potatoes are hot.

Transfer the potatoes to the baking pan and bake for 25 to 30 minutes or until the potatoes are golden and almost tender. Add the balsamic vinegar and salt and pepper to taste; toss well. Bake 5 to 8 minutes longer, or until the potatoes are tender. Serves 6

roasted new potato salad

This roasted potato salad is one of my favorites. It goes well with grilled steak, burgers, chicken, about anything you would serve to your friends on a beautiful summer evening. I bet you will really like it. —MG

3 pounds red new potatoes, scrubbed
About ⅔ cup coarse salt
2 tablespoons dry white wine
¾ cup plus 2 tablespoons extra-virgin olive oil
3 tablespoons cider vinegar
4 shallots, coarsely chopped
3 tablespoons fresh tarragon leaves
2 tablespoons Dijon mustard
Freshly black ground pepper to taste
3 scallions, green parts only, chopped
½ bunch fresh flat-leaf parsley, chopped

Preheat the oven to 400°F.

Place the potatoes in a baking pan large enough to hold them in a single layer and pour the coarse salt generously over them. Roast until tender but firm when pierced, 50 to 60 minutes, depending on the size of the potatoes.

Remove the potatoes from the oven and, using two pot holders, rub off the excess salt from each potato. Place on a cutting board and cut into narrow slices. (If the potatoes are still very hot, hold them with a pot holder or paper towel as you slice.) Transfer the slices to a bowl. Immediately drizzle the white wine, extra-virgin olive oil, and 1 tablespoon of the vinegar over the hot potatoes. Toss gently and set aside.

Combine the shallots and tarragon in a food processor fitted with a metal blade and process to chop finely. Add to the potatoes and toss gently.

Whisk together the ¾ cup olive oil, the remaining 2 tablespoons vinegar, and the mustard in a small bowl. Season with pepper. Pour the dressing over the potatoes, cover the bowl with plastic wrap, and refrigerate for at least 1 hour or up to 2 days.

Remove the potato salad from the refrigerator. Add the scallions and parsley and toss gently. Taste and adjust the seasonings. If desired, let stand for about 1 hour before serving. Transfer to a serving bowl and serve.   Serves 8

grilled corn
with jalapeño citrus butter

Cooking corn on the grill is a blast, and in my experience, each time we do it, it turns into a social event. Nobody cares when I grill fish or burgers. But throw a few ears of corn on the grill, and I suddenly draw a crowd. Maybe it's the aroma when the jalapeño citrus butter hits the hot rack. *Yum!* —LG

8 tablespoons (1 stick) unsalted butter
¼ cup orange juice concentrate
Juice of 1 lime
2 tablespoons molasses
¼ cup chopped fresh cilantro (optional)
4 tablespoons seeded and minced jalapeño peppers
12 ears very fresh corn, shucked
Salt and freshly ground black pepper

Prepare the gas or charcoal grill to medium-high heat. Clean and oil the rack.

Melt the butter in a heavy saucepan over medium heat. Stir the orange juice concentrate, lime juice, and molasses into the melted butter. Stir constantly until well blended. Remove from the heat and stir in the cilantro, if you desire, and the jalapeños.

Place the corn on the prepared grill rack and cook, turning often, until charred spots appear. Brush the corn generously with the citrus butter. Cover the grill and cook for 2 to 3 minutes. Place the corn on a platter and brush with the remaining citrus butter. Serve immediately with salt and pepper to taste.   Serves 6 to 12

ben's peppery potato wedges

This is one of my brother-in-law's stock recipes. Ben likes things *hot*! I serve these with ranch dressing for dipping to offset the cayenne pepper. Ben eats them with Tabasco—go figure. —LG

4 medium russet potatoes, scrubbed
2 tablespoons olive oil
1 teaspoon coarse salt
1 teaspoon freshly ground black pepper
¼ teaspoon cayenne pepper

Preheat the oven to 450°F.

Cut each potato lengthwise into 8 wedges. Toss the wedges in a bowl with the olive oil, salt, black pepper, and cayenne pepper until well coated.

Generously oil a shallow baking pan and place the potato wedges, one cut side down, in the pan. Tightly cover the pan with aluminum foil and roast for 10 minutes. Remove the foil and turn the wedges over, placing the other cut side down. Roast for 10 minutes, uncovered. Turn the wedges again and roast for 10 minutes more, or until nicely browned.   Serves 8

heirloom tomato and haricots verts antipasto

Although technically the word *antipasto* means "before the meal," I like this antipasto plated as a cool side with the entrée, especially with a mild white fish such as haddock, cod, hake, or flounder. It's good with pasta as long as the pasta is fairly simply prepared. Otherwise there's just too much going on for me to thoroughly appreciate the salad. —LG

4 pounds mixed heirloom tomatoes, coarsely chopped

1 pound cherry or grape tomatoes, halved

1 pound haricots verts, blanched, drained, and cooled

1 cup cubed fresh mozzarella cheese

⅓ cup pitted, chopped kalamata olives

3 ounces sliced turkey pepperoni

12 ounces marinated artichoke hearts, coarsely chopped

Salt and freshly ground black pepper

2 tablespoons red wine vinegar

½ cup olive oil

1 teaspoon whole grain mustard

Evenly distribute the heirloom tomatoes, grape tomatoes, and haricots verts on a large serving platter. Scatter the mozzarella, olives, turkey pepperoni, and artichokes over the tomatoes and beans. Grind plenty of pepper over the salad.

Whisk together the vinegar, olive oil, mustard, and salt and pepper to taste. Dress the salad and serve at room temperature. Serves 12

corn pudding with fresh basil

As I mentioned before, this pudding pairs extremely well with the grilled spareribs (see page 130) and Roasted New Potato Salad (page 150). It has been served many times at both my house and Linda's. —MG

4 cups fresh corn kernels (from 6 ears)
1 cup packed fresh basil leaves, torn roughly
3 tablespoons all-purpose flour
¼ teaspoon salt
1 tablespoon sugar
1 cup milk
1 cup heavy cream
4 large eggs, lightly beaten

Place the rack in the middle of the oven and preheat the oven to 350°F. Butter a 2½-quart shallow baking dish.

Pulse 2 cups of the corn in a food processor fitted with a metal blade until coarsely chopped. Transfer to a large bowl and stir in the basil, flour, the remaining corn, the salt, and the sugar. Whisk in the milk, cream, and eggs until combined.

Pour the batter into the prepared baking dish and bake until the center is just set, 45 minutes to 1 hour. Let stand for 15 minutes before serving.   Serves 8 to 10

cucumbers with green sour cream–cumin dressing

This is a fantastic summer side that can be made ahead and refrigerated until you are ready to serve.

There's nothing like a fresh cucumber on a hot day. One of my favorite lunches is a cucumber sandwich with loads of mayonnaise, salt, and pepper on plain old, boring white bread. When cucumbers are in season, it seems as if everyone wants to share what's fresh from their gardens. When the season is over, it's over. So I use lots of cukes for a short time. Store-bought waxy, winter cucumbers just don't cut the mustard. —LG

½ cup arugula leaves, stems removed
½ cup baby spinach, stems removed
½ cup sour cream
1 tablespoon ground cumin
Zest of 1 lime, plus wedges for garnish
1 pound very fresh cucumber, peeled and sliced into ¼-inch rounds
Sweet Hungarian paprika

Place the arugula and spinach in a food processor fitted with a metal blade and process until finely chopped. Add the sour cream, cumin, and lime zest. Puree until smooth. Arrange the cucumber slices on a platter and dress with the sour cream mixture. Garnish with lime wedges and a sprinkle of paprika. Refrigerate for at least 1 hour and serve cold.   Serves 4

salad of tomato, feta, and basil with kalamata vinaigrette

Not only does this salad taste fresh and cool, but it is beautiful on a plate. I like to serve it with a fish or chicken dish that requires a side of rice. This salad enhances that meal both in taste and color. —LG

2 cups cubed tomatoes
½ cup loosely packed fresh basil leaves, chopped
2 tablespoons olive oil
1 teaspoon red wine vinegar
¼ teaspoon sugar
⅓ cup kalamata olives, pitted and minced
½ cup crumbled feta cheese

Mix the tomatoes and basil by hand in a bowl. In a separate bowl, whisk together the olive oil, vinegar, sugar, and olives until well blended. Pour the oil mixture over the tomato mixture and toss to coat. Toss in the feta cheese and serve at room temperature.   Serves 4

baby peas with mustard, & horseradish, and butter

A quick-and-easy way to prepare a green vegetable. It is really tasty with chicken or fish.
—MG

2 cups fresh new peas (or one 10-ounce package frozen baby peas)
¼ cup water
¼ teaspoon salt, plus more to taste
2½ tablespoons unsalted butter, softened
1 tablespoon finely chopped shallot
2 teaspoons prepared horseradish (not drained)
1 teaspoon whole grain mustard
Freshly ground black pepper

Place the peas, water, and the ¼ teaspoon salt in a 2-quart saucepan, and cook, covered, over moderate heat until tender, 5 to 8 minutes.

Meanwhile, mash together the butter, shallot, horseradish, and mustard in a small bowl. Add salt and pepper to taste.

Drain the peas in a colander and return to the saucepan. Stir in the butter mixture and warm over low heat.   Serves 4

grubbing up the *hannah boden*

My last three idyllic island summers of fantastic food have been abbreviated by my self-imposed sword fishing schedule. As I reached the boat for thirty days at sea, I knew my mother's wasn't the only cooking I'd miss.

I held on to the hope that my old shipmate Ringo would, I hesitate to say, "come to his senses," and join me aboard the *Hannah Boden* for a sword fishing reunion, when what I really mean is that I hoped he would have a lapse in judgment. He did manage to be foolish enough to telephone on sailing day (from a safe distance) and wish us luck. Although Ringo surely intended the good wishes, positive vibes, and prayers he addressed to the *Hannah Boden* to keep us safe in unsafe conditions, to bring the mother lode to our hooks, and to receive record-high prices for our catch, I realized as we headed out that we needed help (of divine-intervention intensity) in the galley. I had assembled an all-ace crew. But we were short one cook. I waited so long to convince Ringo to come that I left the dock with five men, all of whom claimed they could make spaghetti.

So it was agreed that we would all take turns preparing meals aboard the *Hannah Boden*. The process of ordering and putting food and drink aboard is called grubbing up. And around midtrip, you can really see why grubbing up well is important. For instance, years ago, when I had assigned a greenhorn truck driver the duties in the galley, two weeks later and a thousand miles from the grocery store, we were eating tuna casserole for the fifth time and debating angrily the question of who had been responsible for grubbing up. There just isn't a lot you can do with pasta, canned tuna, and potato chips. At the other end of the spectrum was Ringo. My mouth waters remembering his prime rib and baked stuffed shrimp.

This time I had been responsible for provisioning the boat for our monthlong trip offshore. Actually, I made the grocery list, and crew member Nate and his girlfriend, Emily, did the shopping. I figured that if I made the list, we would at least have some staples and enough variety so that any of us could come up with a dinner on our turn.

Well, the revolving chef idea never works out. And this trip was not to be an exception. The first to step up in the galley was Carl. He did an amazing job for a guy I knew as a kid who started working for me at the age of fifteen and who I'd spent various sums of money bailing out of problems arising from shooting game out of season. Carl cooked without complaining (other than lamenting that he wished he'd brought some venison) for three nights. While we enjoyed his roast chicken, mashed potatoes, stuffing, carrots, and gravy, he announced that it was Kenny's turn next.

Kenny began questioning me about ingredients I had ordered, and I answered no to most. I did not buy a turkey, a ham, baked beans . . . but I did have corned beef. And Kenny, being a Newfoundlander, had cut his teeth on boiled dinners. On corned beef night, another crewmate, thirty-nine-year-old Johnny, announced that he was trying cabbage for the first time. He admitted that he had never eaten vegetables other than potatoes and carrots and, in fact, had only recently gone out on the epicurean limb with corn on the cob. This confession may have accomplished Johnny's goal. He was out of the cooking rotation and would wash dishes instead.

As I write this from the captain's chair while we steam toward the fishing grounds, I realize that neither Nate nor Harry has prepared a meal. I'm imagining Nate for tacos, minus tomatoes and lettuce—my inadvertent oversight of anything saladlike on the original grub list. Harry fished with me last season for fifty-six days. All I ever saw him cook was ramen noodles. I like noodles—thank goodness. But I won't have noodles or tacos tonight. Tonight is my turn. I somehow figured myself into the rotation and immediately resented the fact that I had to prepare a meal with such an absolute lack of any ingredients I would normally find in my pantry at home. Come to think of it, this crew would not appreciate most of what's on my recipe cards. Sure, I have cooked at sea before. But that was when I was in my rookie season and didn't know how to cook. Tonight I'll make scallops. Fried. May as well take advantage of the calm seas, I think. Why didn't I put panko bread crumbs on the list? I am imagining what will remain in the larder toward the end of the month. I do have a good Internet connection aboard the *Hannah Boden*. I wonder what cookstr.com suggests for bacon, elbow macaroni, and sardines. The only spices I have aboard are chili powder and celery salt. For someone who considers herself a great cook, I am sort of striking out with the imagination here.

Next trip, we'll be grubbing up in Newfoundland, where we can at least sate Carl's hunger for wild game. I recall leaving Bay Bulls, Newfoundland, years ago with a hind quarter of moose, a neck roast of caribou, and a dozen birds, feathers and all. Of course that was the same extended voyage in which we ran out of just about anything edible, and a few other essentials to boot. We ate swordfish hearts, sautéed. They were great. In light of the fact that the men on that epic journey enjoyed smoking lint from the clothes dryer when the cigarettes were gone, I don't have to wonder why I have never eaten hearts since. With five days behind us, and twenty-five to go, I'm missing Ringo. And yes, I am missing another idyllic island summer and my mother's cooking.

great cole slaw

Cole slaw recipes come and go, and you always find yourself going back to the same old tried-and-true cabbage-and-mayo–based dressing. This slaw is really different! There are countless variations, of course, depending on what I find in the refrigerator. But the one thing I keep repeating is the dressing. That it has no mayonnaise is a plus on those hot, sunny days when you just can't get your crowd to stop playing and come eat. —LG

1 pound shredded green cabbage
1 cup shredded red cabbage
½ cup shredded carrots
½ cup chopped scallions, green parts only
⅓ cup minced crystallized ginger
1 cup blue cheese crumbles
¼ cup olive oil
2 tablespoons cider vinegar
1 teaspoon real maple syrup
1 teaspoon freshly ground black pepper

Mix the green cabbage, red cabbage, carrots, scallions, ginger, and blue cheese by hand in a large bowl. Whisk together the olive oil, vinegar, maple syrup, and pepper. Pour the oil mixture over the cabbage mixture and toss until thoroughly coated. You may have to double the dressing if you desire more.   Serves 8

oven-roasted summer squash

I once looked out my kitchen window to see a deer walking through my yard with a summer squash hanging from the corner of its mouth. I knew that one of my gardening neighbors had been violated. When the goods are ripe, there isn't a fence that'll keep the deer out.

This recipe is quick and easy. And it goes well with everything. As a point of interest, deer do not eat rosemary. —LG

2 pounds yellow summer squash or zucchini
¼ cup olive oil
1 teaspoon coarse salt
Freshly ground black pepper
1 teaspoon minced fresh rosemary

Preheat the oven to 450°F.

Cut the squash into ½-inch-thick rounds. Scatter them over a 17x11-inch rimmed baking sheet. Drizzle the squash with the olive oil and sprinkle with the salt, pepper to taste, and rosemary. Toss by with hand to evenly coat.

Roast, turning occasionally, for about 15 minutes, or until caramelized.   Serves 8

mashed yukon golds
with brown butter and parsley

A simple but delicious way to serve mashed potatoes. The brown butter gives them a special taste. —MG

6 to 8 Yukon gold potatoes, scrubbed
Salt and freshly ground black pepper
6 tablespoons unsalted butter
2 tablespoons fresh flat-leaf parsley finely chopped
2 tablespoons finely chopped fresh chives

Cook the potatoes in boiling water until tender, about 20 minutes. Mash the potatoes, then add salt and pepper to taste.

Melt the butter in a small saucepan over medium heat and cook until it turns a light brown. Add the parsley and chives and stir to combine. To serve, drizzle the butter over the mashed potatoes.   Serves 8

capered new potatoes

These grilled potatoes are ideal as an accompaniment to simple broiled fish or poultry. —MG

1 pound new potatoes, scrubbed well
3 tablespoons capers, rinsed and drained
5⅓ tablespoons unsalted butter, softened
Fresh flat-leaf parsley sprigs

Bring enough salted water to cover the potatoes to a boil. Cook the potatoes, in their skins, for 10 minutes. Drain and leave to cool slightly.

Prepare the gas or charcoal grill to medium-high heat. Clean and oil the rack.

Finely chop the capers and blend with the butter. Make a deep slit in each potato and fill it with the caper butter.

Tightly wrap each potato in separate squares of single-thickness aluminum foil and grill for 10 to 15 minutes. Remove from the foil and serve immediately, garnished with parsley sprigs.   Serves 4 to 6

spinach gratin

I love spinach just about any way you can fix it, but this is a recipe that I often use. It is really special with Nancy's Salmon with Hot Mustard Glaze (page 116). —MG

4 tablespoons (½ stick) unsalted butter

4 cups chopped onions (2 large)

¼ cup all-purpose flour

¼ teaspoon freshly grated nutmeg

1 cup heavy cream

2 cups milk

Five 10-ounce packages (about 3 pounds) chopped spinach, defrosted

1 cup grated Parmesan cheese

1 tablespoon kosher salt

½ teaspoon freshly ground black pepper

½ cup grated Gruyère cheese

Preheat the oven to 425°F.

Melt the butter in a heavy-bottomed sauté pan over medium heat. Add the onions and sauté until translucent, about 15 minutes. Add the flour and nutmeg and cook, stirring, for 2 more minutes. Add the cream and milk and cook until thickened.

Squeeze as much liquid as possible from the spinach and add the spinach to the cream sauce. Add ½ cup of the Parmesan and mix well. Season with the salt and pepper.

Transfer the spinach mixture to a greased 9x13-inch baking dish and sprinkle the remaining ½ cup Parmesan and the Gruyère on top. Bake for 20 minutes, or until hot and bubbly.

Serve immediately.   Serves 8

smoky maple baked beans ✗

Baked beans are normally a winter thing for me. But once or twice each summer we have a week of rain and fog during which the good ol' comfort foods seem right in season. Besides, when the sun comes out, I'll eat these cold. I omit the bacon when certain vegetation friends are around. —LG

1 pound dried navy, great northern, or kidney beans
1 large Vidalia onion, chopped
½ cup real maple syrup
2 tablespoons dark brown sugar
2 tablespoons mustard
2 tablespoons molasses
¼ cup store-bought barbecue sauce
½ pound thick-sliced bacon, coarsely chopped
¼ teaspoon Liquid Smoke
Salt and freshly ground black pepper

Cover the beans with water in a large ovenproof Dutch oven. Bring to a boil over high heat. Reduce the heat and simmer for 30 minutes.

Preheat the oven to 275°F.

Mix the onion, maple syrup, brown sugar, mustard, molasses, barbecue sauce, bacon, and Liquid Smoke in a saucepan and add enough boiling water to stir to a thick, smooth consistency. Pour the mixture into the beans and stir to blend.

Cover the pot and place in the oven. Cook for about 5 hours, or until tender, checking occasionally to see that the beans do not dry out. Add water as necessary. Serve hot.   Serves 12

jeweled rice pilaf with cranberries

This is a good way to perk up white rice. The cranberries add color and make an attractive dish. Serve it with chicken or fish. —MG

2 tablespoons unsalted butter
2 tablespoons finely chopped onion
½ teaspoon minced garlic
1 cup converted or parboiled rice
1½ cups chicken broth, homemade or canned, or water
½ cup dried cranberries
3 fresh flat-leaf parsley sprigs
1 fresh thyme sprig or ½ teaspoon dried thyme
1 bay leaf
Salt and freshly ground black pepper

Melt 1 tablespoon of the butter in a saucepan over low heat and add the onion and garlic. Cook, stirring, until the onion is wilted. Add the rice and stir briefly until the grains are coated with the butter. Stir in the chicken broth, making sure there are no lumps in the rice. Add the cranberries, parsley, thyme, and bay leaf. Bring to a boil, cover with a tight-fitting lid, and simmer for 17 minutes.

Uncover the saucepan and remove and discard the parsley, thyme, and bay leaf. Stir in the remaining 1 tablespoon butter, and season with salt and pepper. If the rice is not to be served immediately, keep it covered in a warm place.   Serves 4

orange rice with almonds

This is a tasty orange rice that I have served with Flounder Florentine (page 115). Fresh garden peas would be a good addition. —MG

4 tablespoons (½ stick) unsalted butter
½ cup chopped celery
¼ cup chopped scallions, green parts only
1 cup long-grain rice
1 cup fresh orange juice
1 cup water
1 teaspoon salt
1 teaspoon freshly grated orange zest
1 orange, peeled, seeded, and cut into small pieces
¼ cup slivered almonds

Heat the butter in a saucepan over medium heat and add the celery and scallions. Sauté until tender, 4 to 5 minutes. Add the rice and brown lightly, stirring frequently, for another 4 to 5 minutes. Add the orange juice, water, salt, and orange zest. Heat the mixture to boiling, cover, and simmer for 25 minutes, or until the rice is tender and the liquid is absorbed. Gently stir in the orange pieces and almonds and serve immediately.   Serves 4

rosemary polenta

Another creation from the Inn at Isle au Haut, this polenta dish is a nice accompaniment to beef. In summer there's no shortage of fresh rosemary on our island, so it gets included in many recipes. Polenta is not part of my usual fare—sort of the underutilized ingredient in my pantry. But the few times I have prepared this side, I have wondered why I don't do it more often. It's great! —LG

3 tablespoons olive oil
5 tablespoons unsalted butter
2 garlic cloves, finely minced
½ teaspoon crushed red pepper flakes
½ teaspoon minced fresh rosemary
¼ teaspoon coarse salt
¼ teaspoon freshly ground black pepper
1½ cups chicken broth
1 cup half-and-half
1 cup milk
1 cup yellow cornmeal
¼ cup grated Parmesan cheese
Flour for dusting

Heat 2 tablespoons of the olive oil and 4 tablespoons of the butter in a medium saucepan over medium heat. Add the garlic, red pepper flakes, rosemary, salt, and pepper and sauté for 1 minute. Add the chicken broth, half-and-half, and milk and bring to a boil. Remove from the heat and gradually whisk the cornmeal into the hot milk. Return the pan to the heat and cook over low heat, stirring constantly, until thickened. Remove from the heat again and stir in the Parmesan. Spread the mixture into a 11x7x2-inch pan. Refrigerate for 2 hours, or until firm.

Cut the cold polenta into 8 squares. Cut the squares into triangles. Dust each triangle with flour.

Heat the remaining 1 tablespoon olive oil and 1 tablespoon butter in a nonstick skillet over medium heat. Fry the triangles in batches, turning once, until golden brown and warmed through, about 3 minutes per side.   Serves 8

grilled eggplant and zucchini with tangerine balsamic dressing

In the height of summer, we spark up the grill whenever possible. Not only is it great to cook outside, but it's even better not to heat up the kitchen with my old Glenwood range. I tend to grill seasonal veggies year-round and have oodles of variations for ways to dress them up or down. In my opinion, zucchini and eggplant always *need* a little jazzing up. And this tangerine balsamic dressing is superb. —LG

1 medium eggplant, sliced lengthwise to a thickness of ½ inch

2 medium zucchini, sliced lengthwise to a thickness of ½ inch

2 tablespoons olive oil

Salt and freshly ground black pepper

for the tangerine balsamic dressing

¼ cup olive oil

2 tablespoons balsamic vinegar

2 tablespoons fresh tangerine juice

¼ teaspoon whole grain mustard

Prepare the gas or charcoal grill to medium-high heat. Clean and oil the rack.

Brush the eggplant and zucchini slices generously with the 2 tablespoons olive oil. Sprinkle with salt and pepper to taste. Cook on the grill, turning once, until just tender, but not mushy, about 10 minutes total. Remove to a platter.

To make the dressing, whisk the olive oil, vinegar, tangerine juice, and mustard until well blended. Dress the grilled eggplant and zucchini slices to taste. Serve warm or at room temperature.   Serves 4

yellow rice, sweet corn, and black bean salad

This is a fantastic summer side that goes well with just about anything. It's a great addition to a pig roast or picnic. —LG

4 cups cooked yellow rice, cooled

4 ears fresh corn, cooked, cooled, and kernels cut from the cob

One 14½-ounce can black beans, drained

¼ cup finely chopped roasted red pepper

¼ cup finely chopped green bell pepper

3 tablespoons finely chopped scallions, green parts only

½ teaspoon ground cumin

Favorite store-bought vinaigrette (see Note)

Stirring with a wooden spoon, combine the yellow rice, corn, black beans, red pepper, green bell pepper, and scallions, being careful to not mush the beans. Whisk the cumin into the vinaigrette. Dress the salad lightly with the vinaigrette. The salad can be stored and refrigerated in an airtight container for 3 or 4 days. Serve at room temperature.   Serves 8

note: *If you have don't have any store-bought dressing on hand, make your own vinaigrette with olive oil and vinegar.*

dorothy's french baguettes

One morning I decided to make a lobster stew, because I had lobster left over from the night before. I asked our friends Dorothy Graf and her sister, Betty Pojak, to join Jim and me for dinner that evening. They accepted, and Dorothy decided to bring along a French baguette to go with the meal. Wow! What a great combination. She was kind enough to give me a lesson. —MG

1 package (2¼ teaspoons) active dry yeast
   (not rapid yeast)
1 tablespoon sugar
Scant 1 tablespoon salt
2½ cups warm water
7 cups all-purpose flour
2 large egg yolks, lightly beaten

note: *The loaves can be wrapped in aluminum foil and then frozen. When ready to serve, place the frozen baguette on a cookie sheet in a cold oven, turn on the oven to 400°F, and heat for 10 to 12 minutes.*

Dissolve the yeast, sugar, and salt in the warm water in a large bowl.

Add 2 to 3 cups of the flour to the yeast water and beat with a wooden spoon for 30 seconds to 1 minute. (This activates the gluten, and it is essential.)

Turn the dough out onto a work surface and knead by hand for 10 minutes, adding flour, ¼ cup at a time. I set the timer; then I don't have to watch the clock.

Place the dough in a greased bowl with a lid and let it rise to double in a warm place (80°F, for about 2 hours).

Turn the dough out onto the work surface and punch down and shape it into 4 loaves. Place the loaves in four greased baguette pans. Make 4 or 5 slits with a sharp knife on the top of each baguette and brush with the egg yolks. Place in a warm spot and let the loaves rise to double. This may take up to 1 hour.

Meanwhile, preheat the oven to 450°F.

Place the pans in the oven and bake for 15 minutes. Slide the loaves from the pans and bake for another 10 to 15 minutes, watching carefully so they do not burn (see Note).   Makes 4 baguettes

something sweet

mini cannolis
with crystallized ginger,
orange zest, and blueberries

This cannoli recipe didn't originally call for blueberries, but when they're in season in Maine, we use them. And honestly, if I'm picking them myself, I don't usually get more than a handful, so I can toss my entire harvest into about any recipe. Blueberries work amazingly well in this recipe. —LG

2 pounds fresh ricotta cheese
2 cups confectioners' sugar, plus more for dusting
1 cup mascarpone cheese
2 tablespoons freshly grated orange zest
½ teaspoon pure vanilla extract
½ cup crystallized ginger, minced
4 ounces semisweet chocolate, finely chopped
½ cup very small fresh Maine blueberries
24 store-bought mini cannoli shells

Beat the ricotta, confectioners' sugar, mascarpone, orange zest, and vanilla in a large bowl with an electric mixer on medium-high speed just until blended. Fold in the ginger, chocolate, and blueberries. Refrigerate in an airtight container until ready to use for as long as 1 week.

To serve, put the filling in a pastry bag and, using a large diameter round or star tip, pipe it into a cannoli shell, from both ends of the shell, until full. Repeat with the remaining shells. Dust with confectioners' sugar and serve immediately.   Serves 12

lemon-blueberry mousse tart

This recipe was generously shared by my friend Diana Santospago of the Inn at Isle au Haut. It was served for dessert at my very first dining experience at the inn and is one of many reasons I keep going back. Nobody does it like Diana when it comes to the kitchen. And she promises this is foolproof. (She knows me too well!) This is a dessert for a special summer family gathering. You will, however, need to plan in advance and make it a day ahead. —LG

for the crust

1½ cups walnuts or almonds, toasted

¼ cup sugar

4 tablespoons (½ stick) unsalted butter, melted

for the lemon curd

2¼ cups sugar

2 tablespoons cornstarch

1 tablespoon freshly grated lemon zest

1 cup fresh lemon juice

4 large eggs

4 large egg yolks

12 tablespoons (1½ sticks) unsalted butter

⅓ teaspoon salt

———

1 pint (2 cups) fresh Maine blueberries

for the mousse

5 tablespoons warm water

4 teaspoons unflavored gelatin

Lemon curd (above)

6 large egg whites

¾ cup sugar

1½ cups heavy cream

———

Lemon twists

Fresh mint sprigs

Preheat the oven to 350°F. Grease an 8-inch-diameter springform pan.

To make the crust, grind the walnuts with the sugar in a food processor fitted with a metal blade. Add the butter and pulse to combine. Let cool in the refrigerator for 30 minutes.

Press the cooled crumbs evenly on the bottom of the prepared pan. Bake for 12 minutes, or until light colored. Set aside and cool completely.

To make the lemon curd, whisk the sugar and cornstarch in a heavy saucepan over medium heat. Add the lemon zest and lemon juice gradually, whisking until the cornstarch is dissolved. Whisk in the whole eggs and egg yolks. Add the butter and salt, and cook over medium heat, whisking until the mixture boils and thickens, about 12 minutes. Pour the mixture into a bowl and press plastic wrap on the surface to prevent a skin from forming. Refrigerate for 4 hours.   Serves 12

Spread the cooled crust with ¾ cup of the cold lemon curd. Scatter over the blueberries. Set aside.

To make the mousse, combine the water and gelatin in a small saucepan and let stand until the gelatin softens, about 15 minutes. Warm the mixture over low heat until the gelatin dissolves; do not boil. In a separate saucepan, warm another ¾ cup of the lemon curd over low heat. Whisk the gelatin into the warm curd.

Gradually whisk the gelatin-curd mixture into the remaining cold curd. Beat the egg whites into soft peaks in a medium bowl with an electric mixer on high speed, gradually adding the sugar. Fold the egg whites into the curd mixture in three additions. Beat the cream to soft peaks in a medium bowl. Fold the whipped cream into the mousse in three additions.

Pour the mousse over the blueberries and refrigerate until firm, at least 8 hours. Run a knife around the edges of the pan and loosen the tart from the pan. Garnish with lemon twists and fresh mint sprigs, and serve.   Serves 6

cinnamon-blueberry ice cream

According to my taste buds, all of the best blueberry pie recipes call for a bit of cinnamon and citrus. And blueberry pie à la mode is best with cinnamon ice cream. So why not combine the concepts into one rich dessert? All we're missing here is the crust! —LG

3 cups whole milk
1½ cups sugar
1 cup heavy cream
6 cinnamon sticks
2 whole cloves
⅛ teaspoon salt
12 large egg yolks
Zest of 1 navel orange
3 cups fresh Maine blueberries

Combine the milk, 1 cup of the sugar, the cream, cinnamon, cloves, and salt in a heavy saucepan. Bring to a low simmer over medium heat. In a large bowl, whisk the egg yolks and the remaining ½ cup sugar until well blended. Whisk into the hot mixture a bit at a time, stirring constantly over low heat, until the mixture thickens to a custard consistency.

Cool quickly by setting the pan in a large ice water bath for 30 minutes, stirring often. Cover and refrigerate for 8 hours or overnight.

Strain the custard into a large bowl. Fold in the orange zest and blueberries. Pour the custard into an ice cream maker and process according to the manufacturer's instructions. Freeze in a covered container for up to 1 month.   Serves 8 to 10

key lime rum cake

This is a nice recipe for a crowd—it serves twelve. I can't wait for Alden Leeman, Linda's best friend, to come to the island, because he has a fondness for Mount Gay rum. As everyone on the island knows, Alden is a famous sword fishing captain and Linda's mentor. He will like this cake! —MG

3 cups all-purpose flour

½ teaspoon baking powder

½ cup vegetable shortening

½ pound (2 sticks) unsalted butter

2 cups sugar

5 large eggs

3 tablespoons rum (I like Mount Gay)

2 teaspoons Key lime juice

1 tablespoon Key lime zest

1½ teaspoons pure vanilla extract

1 cup milk

for the glaze

¼ cup sugar

4 tablespoons (½ stick) unsalted butter

2 tablespoons Key lime juice

3 tablespoons Mount Gay rum

Preheat the oven to 325°F. Grease and flour a 10-inch tube pan.

Stir the flour and baking powder together in a mixing bowl.

Cream the shortening, butter, and sugar in a large mixing bowl until light and fluffy. Beat in the eggs, one at a time, until the mixture is light colored. Stir in the rum, lime juice, lime zest, and vanilla until thoroughly blended. Stir in the flour mixture, alternating with the milk in three additions. Pour the batter into the prepared pan.

Bake for about 90 minutes, or until a toothpick inserted into the center comes out clean.

Meanwhile, to make the glaze, cream the sugar and butter in a small saucepan over medium heat until light colored and fluffy. Stir in the lime juice until evenly blended. Bring to a boil, stirring constantly. Remove from the heat and stir in the rum.

Cool the cake in the pan for 10 minutes. Turn it out onto a wire rack or serving plate. While the cake is still warm, use a toothpick to prick the top all over. Pour the glaze evenly over the top of the cake so it drizzles down the sides. Cool the cake completely before serving.   Serves 12

steamed raspberry pudding with hard sauce

When Maine raspberries are in season, make this steamed raspberry pudding, invite some friends over, and share it with them. They will be thrilled to be invited. Our season is never long enough—the month of July is really pushing it. —MG

1½ cups sugar
¾ cup vegetable shortening
4 large eggs, lightly beaten
3 cups milk
4½ cups all-purpose flour
Dash of salt
3 to 4 cups fresh Maine raspberries (according to taste)

for the hard sauce
8 tablespoons (1 stick) unsalted butter, softened
2 cups confectioners' sugar
1 teaspoon pure vanilla extract
Juice of 1 lemon

Cream the sugar and shortening in a large bowl with an electric mixer on medium-high speed until well combined. Add the beaten eggs. Alternate adding the milk and flour in three additions, beating after each addition. Stir in the salt and raspberries. Transfer the mixture to a stainless steel or any other bowl that can stand being in boiling water.

Place a folded towel in the bottom of a large sauce pan. Place the bowl in the pan and add boiling water halfway up the sides of the bowl. Cover the bowl and steam the pudding for about 1 hour or until the pudding is firm to the touch and a skewer placed in the center comes out clean. Cool in the covered bowl for 15 minutes, then unmold onto a platter or plate.

Meanwhile, to make the hard sauce, beat the butter and confectioners' sugar together in a medium bowl with an electric mixer on medium speed until smooth. Stir in the vanilla and lemon juice. Set aside at room temperature until ready to serve on the warm pudding.

When ready to serve, reheat the pudding in the steamer or a microwave, if necessary. Cut the pudding into wedges and serve the hard sauce on the side.   Serves 6 to 8

chocolate mousse
with blueberries

Chocolate mousse is a very popular dessert in the warm summer months, when our lovely Maine blueberries are in season. You can make the mousse and chill it overnight, leaving the next day to get the main course together. —MG

One 12-ounce package semisweet chocolate chips
6 tablespoons water
6 tablespoons sugar
6 large eggs, separated
1 cup heavy cream, whipped
1 pint (2 cups) fresh Maine blueberries

Melt the chocolate chips, water, and sugar in a saucepan over low heat. Cool.

Using a whisk, beat the egg whites in a bowl until stiff. In a separate bowl, beat the egg yolks very well. Add the cooled chocolate to the yolks and beat well. Fold the beaten egg whites into the chocolate mixture. Add the whipped cream. Chill, covered, overnight.

Serve in individual goblets. Sprinkle a few blueberries over the top of each serving.   Serves 8 to 10

lemon meringue pie
with mixed nut crust

Anyone who knows me has heard the story of my siblings and me growing up on a dairy farm in Winslow, Maine. Mom was up every Sunday morning very early so that she could get the baking done for the week (and the goodies lasted only two days). She often made a lemon meringue pie that we devoured before she even had a chance to put it on the table. (My big brothers had large appetites for anything sweet.) A beautiful lemon meringue pie every Sunday during the summer season was a must in our house. Thank you, Mom! —MG

for the mixed nut crust

8 to 10 whole graham crackers (1 wrapped packet), coarsely broken

¼ cup coarsely chopped pecans

¼ cup coarsely chopped walnuts

3 tablespoons sugar

5 tablespoons unsalted butter, melted

for the lemon filling

1½ cups sugar

¼ cup all-purpose flour

⅛ teaspoon salt

1½ cups boiling water

4 large eggs

2 tablespoons unsalted butter

1 teaspoon freshly grated lemon zest

6 tablespoons fresh lemon juice

for the meringue

4 large egg whites

Pinch of salt

½ cup sugar

Preheat the oven to 350°F.

To make the crust, process the graham crackers, pecans, and walnuts to fine crumbs in a food processor fitted with a metal blade. Add the sugar and pulse to mix. With the motor running, add the butter until absorbed.

Press the graham cracker mixture over the bottom and up the sides of a 9-inch pie plate. Bake for 10 to 12 minutes, or until nearly set. The crust will firm up as it cools. Cool on a wire rack. Raise the oven temperature to 450°F.

To make the filling, whisk together the sugar, flour, and salt in a saucepan. Pour on the boiling water. Stir over low heat for about 5 minutes, or until the mixture has thickened and no longer tastes starchy.

Slightly beat the eggs in a bowl. Pour the hot mixture over them, stirring all the while. Return the mixture to the saucepan and place over low heat. Stir and cook for about 2 minutes, or just until the mixture thickens. Remove from the heat and stir in the butter, lemon zest, and lemon juice. Cool slightly before pouring the filling into the prepared crust.

To make the meringue, beat the egg whites and salt in a medium bowl with an electric mixer on high speed until stiff but not dry. Beat in the sugar, 1 tablespoon at a time, beating thoroughly after each addition. It takes a long time of beating to dissolve the sugar, and when it isn't dissolved, it turns into syrup and forms bubbles.

Cover the filling with the meringue, starting from the outside edges and working toward the center. Swirl the meringue a little, but have the top fairly smooth, or it will brown unevenly. Be sure the meringue touches the edges all around, or it may shrink or slip when cut. Bake for 4 to 5 minutes, until lightly browned, and watch it carefully. Cool at room temperature, then place in the refrigerator until chilled and ready to serve.   Serves 8

mile-high strawberry pie

If you ever have a chance to taste a Maine strawberry, you are in for the treat of your life. The berries are luscious, sweet, and smell so good. Our season is short, but everyone loads up on the berries if they can. In strawberry season, you can smell sensational strawberry pies all over the island. —MG

for the crust
One 5-ounce package shortbread cookies
2 tablespoons sugar
2 tablespoons unsalted butter, cut into pieces

for the strawberry filling
2 pounds strawberries, hulled
¾ cup sugar
⅓ cup fresh lemon juice
1 envelope unflavored gelatin
Lightly sweetened whipped cream

Position the rack in the middle of the oven and preheat the oven to 350°F.

To make the crust, put the cookies in a food processor fitted with a metal blade and pulse to fine crumbs, then pulse in the sugar and butter until combined. Press the crumb mixture evenly onto the bottom of a 9-inch pie plate. Bake until golden, about 15 minutes. Transfer to a wire rack to cool.

To make the filling, select 20 large strawberries as close to the same size as possible and set aside. Cut the remaining strawberries into a ¼-inch dice and toss with the sugar and lemon juice. Let stand, stirring occasionally, for 30 minutes. Drain the strawberries in a sieve set into a large glass measuring cup. Add enough water to the drained liquid to measure 2 cups. Transfer the liquid to a medium saucepan and reserve the strawberries.

Sprinkle the gelatin over the strawberry liquid and let it soften for 1 minute. Bring the sauce to a bare simmer, stirring until the gelatin has dissolved. Add the diced strawberries and transfer to a metal bowl set into an ice bath. Let cool for 20 to 30 minutes, stirring frequently.

Spoon ½ cup of the filling into the pie crust and arrange the reserved whole berries, stem sides down, on the filling. Spoon the remaining filling over and between the strawberries. Chill the pie until the filling is set, at least 4 hours and up to 1 day. Serve with lightly sweetened whipped cream.   Serves 8

blueberry cheesecake

The blueberry season in Maine usually runs from the end of July, through August, and into the first two weeks of September. During that time I make a pie at least once a week, depending on whether Aubrey and Addy, my darling grandchildren, are on the island. They *love* blueberry pie. They also love blueberry muffins, blueberry pancakes, anything blueberry. When we are expecting other guests (which is most of the time), I like to make this blueberry cheesecake. —MG

for the crust
8 tablespoons (1 stick) unsalted butter
1½ cups graham cracker crumbs
2 tablespoons sweet sherry

for the blueberry filling
2 cups fresh ricotta cheese
⅔ cup plain yogurt
⅓ cup sugar
1 tablespoon fresh lemon juice
2 large eggs, separated
2 pints (4 cups) fresh Maine blueberries
1 tablespoon unflavored gelatin
2 tablespoons water

for the topping
¼ cup red currant jelly

Mint sprigs
⅔ cup heavy cream, whipped

Grease a 9-inch round, loose-bottomed cake pan.

To make the crust, melt the butter in a saucepan over medium heat. Stir in the graham cracker crumbs and sherry. Mix well. Press the graham cracker mixture onto the base of the cake pan. Place the pan in the refrigerator to firm.

To make the filling, beat the ricotta, yogurt, ¼ cup of the sugar, lemon juice, and egg yolks by hand in a bowl. Gently stir in ⅔ cup of the blueberries.

Sprinkle the gelatin over the water in a small bowl and leave to soften for 2 to 3 minutes. Place the bowl in a saucepan of hot water and stir the mixture until dissolved and quite hot. Stir into the ricotta mixture.

Briskly whisk the egg whites with the remaining sugar until firm and smooth. Fold the beaten egg whites into the ricotta mixture with a large metal spoon, then spoon the filling onto the crumb base. Let set in the refrigerator for 2 to 3 hours.

To make the topping, melt the jelly in a small saucepan over low heat; do not boil. Stir in the remaining blueberries. Mix well, spread over the cheesecake, and chill for a minimum of 2 hours. Decorate with mint sprigs and serve with whipped cream.   Serves 8 to 10

honeydew
with lemon-mint cream

The lemon-mint cream is a nice way to jazz up melon. This is a great addition to a brunch, and works well as a light dessert. —LG

½ cup heavy cream
1 tablespoon sugar
1½ teaspoons minced fresh mint leaves
Zest of 1 lemon
1 ripe honeydew melon, seeded and cut into 6 serving-size wedges
1 cup fresh Maine blueberries (optional)

Beat the cream and sugar with an electric mixer on high speed until firm peaks form. Fold the mint and lemon zest into the whipped cream. Top the melon wedges with a dollop of minted cream and garnish with blueberries, if desired. Serve immediately.   Serves 6

chewy raspberry brownies

I think most people love brownies. I know I do. My daughter Rhonda makes this recipe. The brown sugar and the raspberry liqueur give the brownies a wonderful taste. —MG

10 ounces bittersweet chocolate

3 ounces semisweet chocolate

2½ ounces unsweetened chocolate

½ pound (2 sticks) unsalted butter

1 cup granulated sugar

¾ cup firmly packed dark brown sugar

3 large eggs

¾ cup raspberry liqueur, such as Chambord

2 teaspoons pure vanilla extract

1½ cups all-purpose flour

¼ teaspoon salt

2 tablespoons confectioners' sugar

Preheat the oven to 350°F. Butter a 13×9×2-inch baking pan.

Coarsely chop the bittersweet chocolate, semisweet chocolate, and unsweetened chocolate. In the top of a double boiler, melt the chocolates with the butter, stirring occasionally, until smooth. Remove the top portion of the double boiler and cool the mixture to lukewarm, about 10 minutes.

Beat the granulated sugar, brown sugar, and eggs in a large bowl with an electric mixer on high speed until thick and light colored, about 5 minutes. Beat in the liqueur and vanilla. Add the chocolate mixture and mix until well blended. With the mixer at low speed, beat in the flour and salt just until combined.

Pour the batter into the prepared pan and smooth the surface with a rubber spatula. Bake for 25 to 30 minutes, or until a toothpick inserted 2 inches from the center comes out slightly moist. Cool the brownies in the pan on a wire rack. When completely cool, cut into 20 bars. Place the confectioners' sugar in a sieve and dust the tops of the brownies after cutting.   Makes 20 brownies

old-fashioned peanut butter cookies

My grandmother used to make these cookies about once a week. She gave me the job of making crisscross marks with fork tines. Standing on a chair, pulled up to the counter (with one of her aprons wrapped around me), I felt pretty important. What is better than eating these cookies on a warm summer morning, wishing that you could have just one more? —MG

½ cup smooth peanut butter

8 tablespoons (1 stick) unsalted butter, softened

½ cup granulated sugar, plus more for crisscrossing the cookies

½ cup firmly packed light brown sugar

½ teaspoon baking soda

¼ teaspoon salt

1 large egg

½ teaspoon pure vanilla extract

1¼ cups all-purpose flour

Preheat the oven to 375°F.

Beat the peanut butter and butter in a large mixing bowl with an electric mixer on medium to high speed for 30 seconds. Add the granulated sugar, brown sugar, baking soda, and salt. Beat until combined, scraping down the sides of the bowl occasionally. Beat in the egg and vanilla until combined. Gradually beat in as much flour as you can with the mixer. Stir in any remaining flour. Cover with plastic wrap and refrigerate the dough for about 1 hour, or until easy to handle.

Shape the dough in to 1-inch balls. Place the balls 2 inches apart on an ungreased cookie sheet. Flatten the cookies by making crisscross marks with fork tines, dipping the fork in granulated sugar between flattening each cookie. Bake for about 8 minutes, or until the edges are lightly browned. Cool on wire racks.   Makes 36 cookies

white chocolate mint brownies

One of my neighbors walked in for a visit right about the time that I was adding the fresh mint to the brownie batter. He looked at me sort of funny and said, "Medicinal, right?" Imagine putting fresh herbs in brownies when it's not illegal. And I can share these with my nephews! —LG

6 ounces unsweetened chocolate, coarsely chopped
8 tablespoons (1 stick) unsalted butter
1 cup all-purpose flour
½ teaspoon baking powder
¼ teaspoon salt
1¼ cups sugar
3 large eggs
2 teaspoons pure vanilla extract
6 ounces white chocolate chips
¼ cup minced fresh mint

Preheat the oven to 325°F. Grease an 8x8-inch baking pan with nonstick cooking spray.

Melt the chocolate and butter in a heavy saucepan over low heat until smooth. Remove from the heat and let cool.

Combine the flour, baking powder, and salt in a small bowl. In a separate bowl, whisk the sugar, eggs, and vanilla until smooth and thick. Whisk in the melted chocolate, and then the flour mixture. Stir in the white chocolate chips and mint.

Spread the batter in the prepared pan. Bake for 30 minutes, or until a toothpick inserted into the center comes out clean. Let cool. Cut and enjoy.   Makes 16 brownies

index

croutons, garlic, and Asiago, romaine salad with, 43

crust, mixed nut, lemon meringue pie with, 190–91

cucumbers with green sour cream-cumin dressing, 158

cumin-sour cream dressing, green, cucumbers with, 158

D

dessert:
blueberry cheesecake, 194–95
chewy raspberry brownies, 197
chocolate mousse with blueberries, 189
cinnamon-blueberry ice cream, 184
honeydew with lemon-mint cream, 196
Key lime rum cake, 186–87
lemon-blueberry mousse tart, 182–83
lemon meringue pie with mixed nut crust, 190–91
mile-high strawberry pie, 192–93
mini cannolis with crystallized ginger, orange zest, and blueberries, 181
old-fashioned peanut butter cookies, 198
steamed raspberry pudding with hard sauce, 188
white chocolate mint brownies, 199

dill, halibut steaks with, 132

dip, dipping sauce:
clam, Schoolhouse shore, 10
crab, Brenda's famous, 22
garlic-wasabi, summer veggie spring rolls with, 86–87
peanut-ginger, grilled swordfish kebabs with, 110–11
spicy yogurt, raw veggies with, 11

Dorothy's French baguettes, 176

doughnuts, Black Dinah Café, 64–65

dressing:
basil-lime, sliced pear and Manchego with, 29
cool guacamole, green salad with, 41
green sour cream-cumin, cucumbers with, 158
kalamata vinaigrette, salad of tomato, feta, and basil with, 159
tangerine and balsamic, grilled eggplant and zucchini with, 173
white anchovy, grilled Caesar salad with, 42
see also dip, dipping sauce; sauce

drizzle, creamy lemon-pepper, mushroom and radish carpaccio with shaved Manchego and, 75

Dr Pepper glaze, grilled spareribs with, 130–31

E

egg(s):
casserole, brunch, 59
Kate's farm stand quiche, 61–62
poached, with mustard hollandaise sauce, 66–67

eggplant:
fritters with tarragon sour cream, 82–83
and zucchini, grilled, with tangerine balsamic dressing, 173

F

fennel, steamed mussels with Pernod and, 102

feta, basil, and tomato salad with kalamata vinaigrette, 159

fish:
cod, coconut panko, with Mexi tartar sauce, 118
flounder Florentine, 115
halibut steaks with dill, 132
halibut with herb sauce, 120
salmon, smoked, spread with rice crackers, 15
salmon with hot mustard glaze, Nancy's, 116
striper ceviche, 96
swordfish, blackened, with blueberry chutney, 112–14
tuna, seared, with sake-soy reduction and fried ginger, 80–81
white anchovy dressing, grilled Caesar salad with, 42
see also shellfish

French:
baguettes, Dorothy's, 176
pancakes, delicately thin, with fresh blueberry syrup, 68

fried ginger, seared tuna with sake-soy reduction and, 80–81

fritters, eggplant, with tarragon sour cream, 82–83

fruit:
honeydew with lemon-mint cream, 196
mango cilantro crème fraîche, lobster cocktail with, 90
mango-tomato chutney, grilled turkey burgers with, 126
orange rice with almonds, 171
orange zest, crystallized ginger, and blueberries, mini cannolis with, 181
pear, sliced, and Manchego with basil-lime dressing, 29
pineapple, grilled, with two dipping sauces, 26–27
tangerine balsamic dressing, grilled eggplant and zucchini with, 173
see also berry(ies); lemon; lime

G

galette, tomato, caramelized onion, and Brie, 49–50

garlic:
-basil butter, baked shrimp with, 88
croutons and Asiago, romaine salad with, 43
-sage hummus, sea-salted pita crisps with, 14
-wasabi dipping sauce, summer veggie spring rolls with, 86–87

gazpacho, Maine shrimp, 33

ginger:
-bran blueberry muffins, 70–71
crystallized, mini cannolis with orange zest, blueberries and, 181